# JOHN PAUL II
# AN INVITATION TO JOY

*Totus Tuus ego sum*
*Et omnia mea Tua sunt.*
*Accipio Te in mea omnia.*
*Praebe mihi cor Tuum,*
*María.*

I belong to you entirely
And all that I possess is yours.
I take you into everything that is mine.
Give me your heart,
Mary.

This prayer of entrustment to the Virgin Mary is the Pope's own adaptation of
two invocations by Saint Louis-Marie Grignion de Montfort (1673–1716).
It is one of the Holy Father's favorites, and he recites it daily.

# AN INVITATION TO JOY

Selections from the writings and speeches of

## HIS HOLINESS JOHN PAUL II

With commentary by Greg Burke

Preface by Archbishop Jorge María Mejía
Archivist and Librarian of the Holy Roman Church

SIMON & SCHUSTER

*in association with*

CALLAWAY EDITIONS
&
LEONARDO PERIODICI

# CONTENTS

Preface by Archbishop Jorge María Mejía

## III
# THE DIGNITY OF THE HUMAN PERSON
*For Life · Human Rights · Solidarity · Freedom*
*Peace & War · Suffering & Evil*
146

## IV
# A LIFETIME OF DEVOTION
200

## Acknowledgments
224

*Frontispiece: Poland, 1987; pages 6–7: Bahia Blanca, Argentina, 1987; pages 8–9: St. Peter's Basilica and Square, Vatican City, Easter Sunday, 1985; pages 10–11: Santiago de Compostela, Spain, 1986; pages 12–13: The Pope blesses the Nativity scene, St. Peter's Basilica, Vatican City, 1985; pages 14–15: St. Peter's Square, Vatican City, Easter Sunday, 1985; pages 16–17: Dominican Republic, 1979; pages 18–19: Ivory Coast, 1982; pages 20–21: The Papal Apartment, Vatican City, 1986*

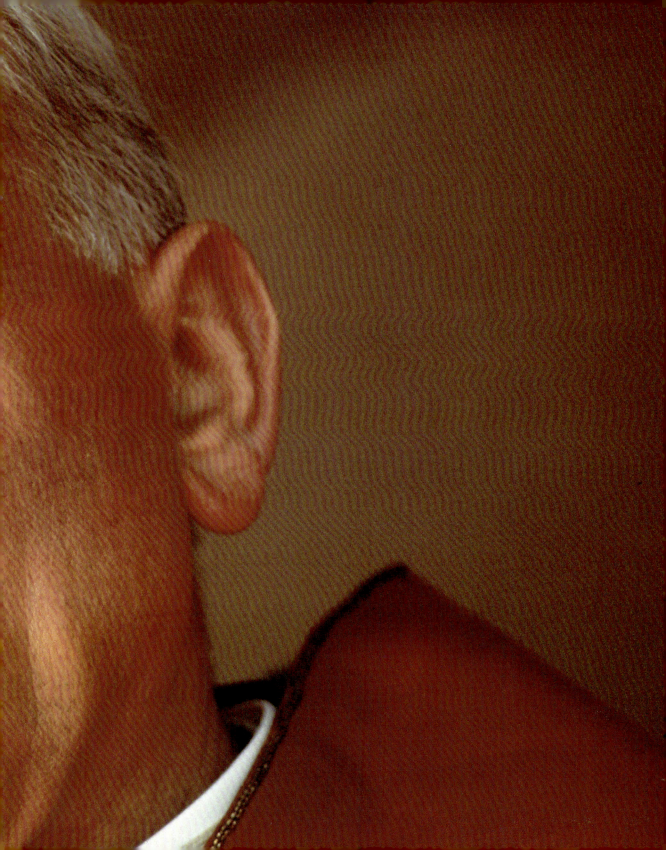

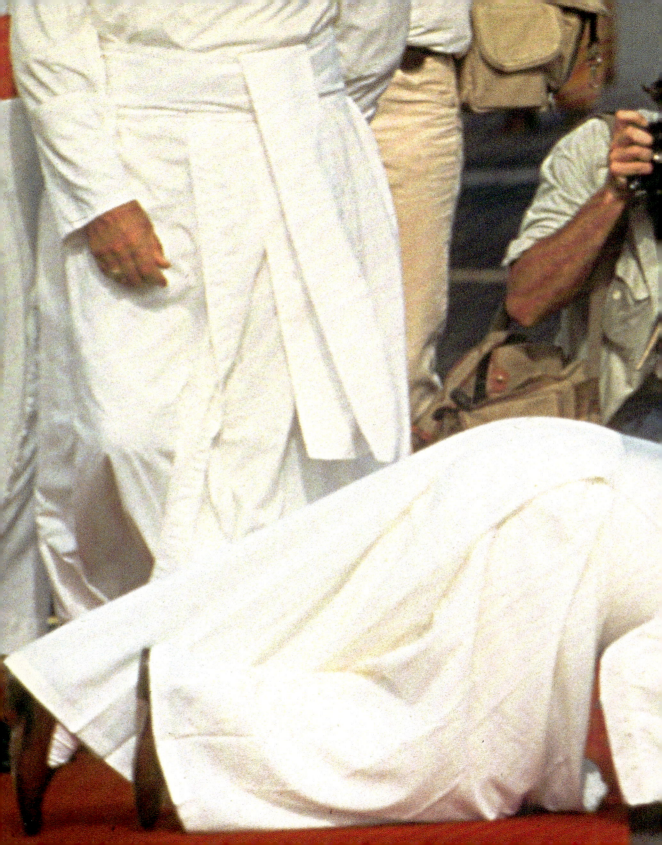

HE TITLE OF THIS BOOK NOT ONLY MENTIONS JOY; it is indeed *An Invitation to Joy*, and thus prompts us to ask, What is the relationship between the Pope and, of all things, joy? The answer is perhaps not immediately apparent from the contents page, which lists the book's main sections as The Human Family, The People of God, The Dignity of the Human Person, and A Lifetime of Devotion. At first, it might be difficult to believe that such categories, rather alien to most of us, could be sources of joy. Some would even say the contrary is true: These titles imply, and sometimes are, real sources of concern rather than joy.

But, reading this book, one is certainly very positively impressed, if not altogether elated, by the pictures and texts of and by the Holy Father. His life and message as presented here truly are an invitation to joy, perhaps even the incarnation of joy. Here is a man, known around the world, who proclaims with gestures and words that life is worth living; that it has a meaning; that it is not closed off between two inscrutable abysses; that it is not inside itself, but is open to others; that love is possible and enriching; that all of us, men and women, whatever the hue of our skins, are called to form a family with God. He proclaims these ideas hold true even if we belong to different churches and different religions; that this family is somehow built upon and brought about by the individual human families into which we are born or that we form on our own. In this sense, we can really become and be called the people of God. If all this is true and somehow made visible and tangible in the Pope's life and message, then there is truly a reason for joy.

*"Trinity in an Apse," from* The Book of Hours of Catherine of Cleves

In a way, it all depends on what we understand joy to be. I daresay it is not feeling all right and happy today and maybe tomorrow and then that is the end of it. Joy is a much deeper sentiment and even perhaps more than a sentiment. Not even a state of mind. A way of being. A kind of second nature. If I am allowed a quotation from the Gospel—which may not be entirely out of order as this book is woven with quotations—I would like to offer one I have always found very impressive. In the Gospel of John, Jesus says: "I have told you this so that my joy may be in you and that your joy may be complete." Two remarkable affirmations in this quotation may enlighten us about the real meaning of joy. The first is the assertion of someone who, even through suffering and death, speaks about joy being his. And second, it seems that when we receive the joy he brings—his joy—then our joy is *complete*. Obviously enough, this goes well beyond superficial happiness or transient, precarious pleasure.

Are we to believe, therefore, that to participate in the fullness of joy we should become Christian and be faithful disciples of Jesus? I am not afraid to affirm such a thing. What is true beyond all doubt is that the man whose life and message are pictured here is an exemplary Christian, a man whose joy seems to be indeed complete.

Although the Pope is not feeling well and sometimes looks as if in pain, he proclaims joy, he radiates joy, he shows the way to joy. We cannot avoid concluding that joy goes well beyond physical fitness, a life of comfort and abundance—what we mean by "feeling well."

Joy comes from harmony, as the ancients used to say, and harmony is here properly applied. Harmony with oneself. Harmony with our fellow human beings. Harmony with the place which is ours in the universe and in history. Harmony with creation and the Creator. Harmony therefore with God and with whomever he sent to restore harmony to a broken world and a broken humanity. We return to Jesus' own statement in the Gospel of John: "[T]hat my joy may be in you and that your joy may be complete."

*An Invitation to Joy*, as seen in the images and words of Pope John Paul II, is an elaboration of this statement. It shows a man who grew up under Nazi oppression, earning his living through hard physical labor to avoid being sent to forced labor in Germany; who at the same time managed to write poetry, participate in theatrical shows, and study philosophy and theology clandestinely because such things were forbidden in occupied Poland. His friends and classmates, Christian and Jewish, disappeared before his eyes. And after this suffering, he found himself and his country sacrificed to another oppression under Communism—and no one could predict for how long.

When we met in Rome in November 1946 at the Angelicum University, I never would have guessed his background. There was nothing of the victim in his attitude. He taught me and our other classmates hope, serenity, and, of course, joy. Then he was only a young student priest, as we all were. Still, we—who knew nothing about war, oppression, and genocide—could already learn from him a lesson for our lives. He would always return to the place he came from—behind the Iron Curtain—while most of the rest of us would return home to a "free" world. Notwithstanding, his person and his message were about joy and complete joy.

Is it because I now look at him from this vantage point that I read the book as an invitation to joy? Perhaps. But I am not alone. I am joined by those who first had the idea of publishing such a collection of images and quotations, and by Greg Burke, who selected the quotations and wrote the commentary for the book. They must all have succumbed to the same impression I had more than fifty years ago.

Is it too much to expect that some of the book's readers, if not all (and why not all?), will succumb to the same kind of joyful fascination?

*Archbishop Jorge María Mejía*
*Archivist and Librarian of the Holy Roman Church, June 1999*

# I
# The Human Family

The Pope preaches one message—love—to the entire world, Catholic and non-Catholic alike. He asks everyone to be bearers of hope in a world frequently filled with desperation; to be men and women of faith in societies that seem to have lost any need for God; and to be channels of love and generosity in an age of unbridled egoism.

*Lyons, France, 1986*

ABOVE: *"Adoration of the Child," from* The Book of Hours of Catherine of Cleves

oung people energize the Pope. He will sing with them, wave his cane for them, and make funny faces at them. While the very presence of young people lifts John Paul II's spirits, he knows how to spread that joy to them as well. He will gladly don a cowboy hat, pick up a hockey stick, or stamp his feet in unison with their cheers and chants. During his travels, his meetings with young people are always the noisiest and the most fun. But along with the shouts and the laughter, the Pope brings a serious message and a heartfelt prayer. The message is always the same: You are the future of the Church; You are the future of the world. And the prayer is always linked to the message: May you have the courage to follow Christ closely at all times during your life.

The Pope continually challenges youth. In 1998, he talked to young Cubans about bravery and commitment; about "the courageous response of people who do not want to let life pass them by but rather seek to shape their own personal history and the history of the society around them." The Pontiff wants that commitment from the young, that whatever path they take in life, they walk as dedicated Christians.

He inaugurated World Youth Day in 1986 to celebrate the faith of young Catholics worldwide, and ever since then, he has either invited young people to Rome or traveled with them on pilgrimages around the globe. The biennial festivities bring together the best elements of a rock concert and a spiritual retreat. John Paul seems to like that combination of high-energy song and dance with the silence of the prayer vigil. Youth, he believes, should learn to enjoy both.

Young people have not only energy but also ideals, and the Pope encourages them in what he calls their "thirst for truth." He views adolescence not as a time to reject religion but as a time to embrace it. "See to it that your youth is not only a purely transitory moment in your lives," he wrote in a 1984 letter, "but realize it fully by remaining united to the word of God, which is always young."

John Paul understands that youth means a time of questions, of looking for direction. He insists—and he used to do so at the top of his lungs—that Christ has the answers. Turn to Jesus, listen to him, and discover the true meaning of your lives, he tells young people, challenging them to foster a prayer life, a sincere dialogue with Jesus Christ.

The Pontiff has frequently focused on the Gospel parable of the rich young man who approaches Christ, tells him that he has lived all the commandments, and asks what more he should do to gain eternal life. Jesus answers that he should sell all his belongings, give his money to the poor, and follow him. The young man goes away sad; he does not want to give up his possessions. The Pope contends that this parable remains valid today, when young people are driven to think that what is important is what they own, what they wear, and how much money they have.

So, when speaking with young people, John Paul pounds away with his countercultural but Gospel-centered message: Leave all those material things that keep your hearts from being free. What is important is love of God and love of neighbor. "You must reflect the light of Christ through your lives of prayer and joyful service to others," the Pope told a youth gathering in St. Louis in January 1999.

For teens and young adults, the Pope is a sign of hope in a world that he acknowledges is often filled with darkness: children who go hungry and die; homeless people; violence in families; sexual abuse; drug abuse that destroys bodies, minds, and hearts. But Christ's light shines brightly through the darkness, and those who remain close to him in prayer come to share in his light, and bring it to others who are lost in the dark. In a world in which many people are slaves to their passions, Christ liberates human souls, lifting them out of their shackles.

John Paul promises that, through Christ, young men and women will not only work toward building a better world, but find the truths and values on which to build their own happiness. "Remember," he says, "Christ is calling you; the Church needs you; the Pope believes in you, and he expects great things of you! . . . Even though you are young, the time for action is now! It is time to let your light shine!"

OVERLEAF: *Lourdes, 1983*

*Sicily, 1993*

The Church entrusts to young people the task of proclaiming to the world the joy which springs from having met Christ. Dear friends, allow yourselves to be drawn to Christ; accept his invitation and follow him. Go and preach the good news that redeems; do it with happiness in your hearts and become communicators of hope in a world which is often tempted to despair.

*Message for World Youth Day, Vatican City, 1993*

*A*s baptized individuals, you bear witness to Christ by your concern for a life that is upright and faithful to the Lord, maintained by means of a spiritual and moral struggle. Faith and moral behavior are linked. In fact, the gift received leads us to a permanent conversion, so that we might imitate Christ and be worthy of the divine promise. The word of God transforms the lives of those who accept it, because it is the rule of faith and action.

*Message for World Youth Day, Paris, 1997*

*T*o all of you, dear young people, who hunger and thirst for truth, the Church offers herself as a traveling companion. She offers the eternal Gospel message and entrusts you with an exalting apostolic task: to be the protagonists of the new evangelization.

*Message for World Youth Day, Vatican City, 1993*

*Vienna, 1983*

OVERLEAF: *St. Peter's Square, Vatican City, Epiphany morning, 1985*

Young people should be helped to discover very early on the value of the gift of self, an essential factor in reaching personal maturity.

*Discourse to Nigerian Bishops Conference, Vatican City, 1998*

What enormous power the prayer of children has! This becomes a model for grown-ups themselves: praying with simple and complete trust means praying as children pray.

*Letter to Children in the Year of the Family, Vatican City, 1994*

Men and women seek God. Young people realize in the depths of their being that this quest is the inner law of their lives. Human beings seek their way in the visible world and, through the visible world, they seek the unseen world at every stage of their spiritual journey.

*Message for World Youth Day, Paris, 1997*

In children there is something that must never be missing in people who want to enter the kingdom of heaven. People who are destined to go to heaven are simple like children, and like children are full of trust, rich in goodness and pure. Only people of this sort can find in God a Father and, thanks to Jesus, can become in their own turn children of God.

*Letter to Children in the Year of the Family, Vatican City, 1994*

*Lodz, Poland, 1987*

OVERLEAF: *Onitsha, Nigeria, 1982*

or John Paul II, the traditional family is at the heart of what he calls the "civilization of love." It is the first school of virtues, of generous self-giving and joy. Parenthood itself is nothing less than a man and a woman sharing in the creative power of God, who is love.

And, if building a family is an imitation of God—if the family is the fundamental cell of society—then breaking one up can only be called evil. The Pope warns that more than love is destroyed when spouses separate; society is damaged as well. He calls upon parents considering divorce to remember their responsibilities to their offspring and to God. For John Paul sees marriage not only as a contract between two people, but also as an accord they have made with God. The marriage bond brings joy, since it is born of the spouses' love for each other, but it also brings obligations. He stresses the importance of prayer both *with* and *for* families. "We need to pray that married couples will love their vocation, even when the road becomes difficult, or the paths become narrow, uphill and seemingly insuperable. We need to pray that, even then, they will be faithful to their covenant with God."

Once, when visiting a Roman parish, John Paul greeted a group of young couples who were preparing people for marriage in the Catholic Church. He recalled how he had had to spend so many years in the seminary to become a priest and lamented that laypeople get very little help in preparing for marriage, which is also a lifelong and demanding commitment. "They used to get this formation in the home, but that is no longer true," he told the married couples. "That is why your work is so important."

John Paul points out that the vast majority of Christians have been called to married life, to fatherhood and motherhood. He links the fourth commandment, "Honor your father and your mother," to Christ's command to love one another, and he says that "to honor," by its nature, suggests an attitude of generosity. Such generosity—the ability to give of oneself—is at the heart of a solid family for John Paul.

His stalwart defense of the traditional family has won the Catholic Church allies among other Christian denominations and also among Jewish leaders. Calling the family "humanity's most precious resource," the International Catholic Jewish Liaison Committee released a joint declaration in 1994 in an effort to make a positive contribution to the United Nations' International Year of the Family. The declaration, echoing much of John Paul's teaching, stated that the family was far more than a legal, social, or economic unit: "For both Jews and Christians, it is a stable community of love and solidarity based on God's covenant. . . . [It is] uniquely suited to teaching and handing on the cultural, ethical, social and spiritual values that are essential for the development and well-being of its members and of society."

While family unity may sometimes seem impossible to achieve, the Pontiff insists that such is not the case and that the world will reap the positive consequences: "The civilization of love is possible; it is not a utopia." ▦

The family, the great workshop of love, is the first school, indeed, a lasting school where people are not taught to love with barren ideas, but with the incisive power of experience. May every family truly rediscover its own vocation to love!

*February 13th Angelus Prayer, Vatican City, 1994*

It is above all in the home that, before ever a word is spoken, children should experience God's love in the love which surrounds them. In the family they learn that God wants peace and mutual understanding among all human beings, who are called to be one great family.

*Message for World Day of Peace, Vatican City, 1996*

Today more than ever, now that the links between the generations are tending to disintegrate, if young people are to develop intellectually, psychologically and spiritually, they need a stable home where they receive affection and where they learn, from the witness of their elders and through education, the necessary values for their personal life and for a harmonious life with all the people who make up society.

*Address to the French Ambassador to the Holy See, Vatican City, 1995*

*Mbanza Congo, Angola, 1992*

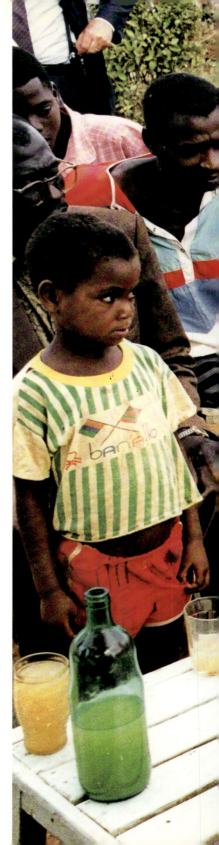

The fostering of authentic and mature communion between persons within the family is the first and irreplaceable school of social life, and an example and stimulus for the broader community relationships marked by respect, justice, dialogue and love.

*Familiaris Consortio (On the Role of the Christian Family in the Modern World), Vatican City, 1981*

The family . . . makes an original contribution in depth to building up the world, by making possible a life that is, properly speaking, human, in particular by guarding and transmitting virtues and values.

*Familiaris Consortio (On the Role of the Christian Family in the Modern World), Vatican City, 1981*

The new evangelization must bring a fuller appreciation of the family as the primary and most vital foundation of society. As the family goes, so goes the nation!

*Homily, St. Louis, Missouri, 1999*

Inspired and sustained by the new commandment of love, the Christian family welcomes, respects and serves every human being, considering each one in his or her dignity as a person and as a child of God.

*Familiaris Consortio (On the Role of the Christian Family in the Modern World), Vatican City, 1981*

*Sistine Chapel, Vatican City, 1997*

Faced with a society that is running the risk of becoming more and more depersonalized and standardized and therefore inhuman and dehumanizing, with the negative results of many forms of escapism—such as alcoholism, drugs and even terrorism—the family possesses and continues still to release formidable energies capable of taking man out of his anonymity, keeping him conscious of his personal dignity, enriching him with deep humanity and actively placing him, in his uniqueness and unrepeatability, within the fabric of society.

*Familiaris Consortio (On the Role of the Christian Family in the Modern World), Vatican City, 1981*

*Rio de Janeiro, 1997*

*"Bambin Gesù" Hospital, Rome, 1988*

very man and every woman was made for love, both to love others and to be loved. "You are worth what your heart is worth," John Paul II told a group of young people in France in 1980. "The entire history of humanity is the history of the need to love, and to be loved." Love, strictly speaking, is something only a human being is capable of, for only he or she can make a gift of self. The Pope believes it is in that giving—and not in the mere pursuit of pleasure—that one finds happiness. While there are different kinds of love, they all have a common thread of the giving of oneself. An individual's fundamental vocation is to love, and his or her life will have meaning inasmuch as it is a gift to others. You "find yourself" by giving yourself.

In 1960, when he was still a young bishop, Karol Wojtyla wrote a book called *Love & Responsibility*. The book deals with his philosophical reflections on Catholic teaching in the light of his experience as a pastor and marriage counselor. An entire chapter analyzes what it means "to use." While the reasoning is at times very complex, the basic message is clear: "To love" is the opposite of "to use."

Wojtyla explains that it is far easier to draw up a standard of sexual morality for Catholics than to persuade people to practice it. The spiritual director, therefore, must know how to justify this standard. Much of *Love & Responsibility* is about sex and the relationship between sex and love. True love, he argues, attempts to make the relationship between a man and a woman completely unselfish, but until then there is a struggle between love and the sexual appetite. "The sexual instinct wants above all to take over, to make use of another person," he writes, "whereas love wants to give, to create a good, to bring happiness."

In his 1994 *Letter to Families,* John Paul refers to the first letter of St. Paul to the Corinthians as a hymn of love. It speaks of a love that is patient and kind and endures all things. St. Paul described how true love is demanding of the one giving love. It is demanding in all human situations, the Pope writes, and even more so in the case of those who are open to the Gospel. While getting along with friends and family members can entail considerable trials, the Gospel takes it a step further and demands that you love your enemies and those who persecute you.

Real love requires that people know how to give of themselves. In the mind of John Paul, selfishness and a false sense of freedom—freedom without responsibility—are what threaten real love and happiness. Promiscuity, he states flatly, has never made men or women

truly happy. Selfishness in all its forms—in individuals, couples, or even nations—is in radical opposition to love, and yet love is more than simply not being selfish. Love is a gift, one that is truly free and unconditional.

Love goes beyond mere physical attraction or instinct, and John Paul stresses the importance of discovering the "inner beauty" of a person one finds attractive. For a love to last, what is needed is a full appreciation of the entire beauty of the person. "When a man and a woman are united by true love, each one takes on the destiny, the future of the other, as his or her own," he maintains. Despite hardship and suffering, each loves the other so that they "have life and have it in abundance." These words of Christ, the Pope tells us, refer to every true love.

Authentic love is not a vague sentiment or a blind passion. It is an inner attitude that involves the whole human being. It is looking at others, not to use them but to serve them. It is the ability to rejoice with those who are rejoicing and to suffer with those who are suffering. It is sharing what one possesses so that no one may continue to be deprived of what he needs. Love, in a word, is the gift of self.

*February 13th Angelus Prayer, Vatican City, 1994*

When one reasons calmly and keeps the ideal in mind, it is not difficult to agree that the permanence of the marriage bond springs from the very essence of love and the family. We love one another truly and absolutely only when we love forever, in joy and in sorrow, in good times and bad.

*July 10th Angelus Prayer, Vatican City, 1994*

May Mary most holy come to the aid of couples in crisis, helping them to rediscover the freshness of their first love.

*July 10th Angelus Prayer, Vatican City, 1994*

*Salvador, Brazil, 1980*

*Warsaw, 1991*

True happiness lies in giving ourselves in love to our brothers and sisters.

*Message to Young People, Camagüey, Cuba, 1998*

Humanity is loved by God! . . . Each Christian's words and life must make this proclamation resound: God loves you, Christ came for you, Christ is for you "the Way, the Truth and the Life!"

*Christifideles Laici (On the Vocation and Mission of the Laity), Vatican City, 1988*

Above all, love is greater than sin, than weakness, than the "futility of creation," it is stronger than death; it is a love always ready to raise up and forgive, always ready to go to meet the prodigal son. . . . In man's history this revelation of love and mercy has taken a form and a name: that of Jesus Christ.

*Redemptor Hominis (The Redeemer of Man), Vatican City, 1979*

Man cannot live without love. He remains a being that is incomprehensible to himself, his life is senseless, if love is not revealed to him, if he does not encounter love, if he does not experience it and make it his own, if he does not participate intimately in it.

*Redemptor Hominis (The Redeemer of Man), Vatican City, 1979*

*Baltimore, 1995*

**G**od created man in his own image and likeness: calling him to existence through love, he called him at the same time for love.

*Familiaris Consortio (On the Role of the Christian Family in the Modern World), Vatican City, 1981*

**G**enuine love . . . is demanding. But its beauty lies precisely in the demands it makes. Only those able to make demands on themselves in the name of love can then demand love from others.

*Message to Young People, Camagüey, Cuba, 1998*

**I**f we do not encounter love, if we do not experience it and make it our own, and if we do not participate intimately in it, our life is meaningless. Without love we remain incomprehensible to ourselves.

*Message to Religious Women, Washington, D.C., 1979*

**I**n our bodies we are a mere speck in the vast created universe, but by virtue of our souls we transcend the whole material world. I invite you to reflect on what makes each one of you truly marvelous and unique. Only a human being like you can think and speak and share your thoughts in different languages with other human beings all over the world, and through that language express the beauty of art and poetry and music and literature and the theater, and so many other uniquely human accomplishments.

And most important of all, only God's precious human beings are capable of loving.

*Homily, New York City, 1995*

henever the progress of women toward equality has been blocked, humanity has suffered what John Paul II calls "spiritual impoverishment." "Women's dignity has often been unacknowledged. . . . They have often been relegated to the margins of society and even reduced to servitude," he wrote in his 1995 *Letter to Women,* adding that the time had come to examine the past with courage and place blame where blame was due.

The Gospel message, the Pope argues, continues to be relevant for setting women free from male exploitation and domination, since the attitude of Christ himself was to transcend the norms of his own culture and treat women with openness and respect. The Pontiff points specifically to Christ not condemning the Samaritan woman at the well who had five husbands, nor the woman caught in adultery. When a public sinner anointed the feet of Jesus with perfumed oil in the house of a Pharisee, the host was shocked. Public opinion had already condemned the woman, but Christ explained, "Her sins, which were many, are forgiven, for she loved much." In saying this, Christ honored the dignity that women have always possessed according to God's plan. How much, the

Pope asks, has Christ's message been heard and acted upon?

John Paul laments the fact that in many parts of the world women are still not fully integrated into the social, political, and economic life of societies, and he calls for "real equality" in every area. By this he means equal pay for equal work, protection for working mothers, fairness in career advancement, and the recognition of everything that is a part of the rights and duties of citizens in a democracy.

The feminist movement, John Paul believes, has been a difficult and complicated journey not without its share of mistakes, including a tendency toward the "masculinization" of women. "But it has been substantially a positive one, even if it is still unfinished due to the many obstacles which, in various parts of the world, still prevent women from being acknowledged, respected, and appreciated in their own special dignity." Progress has to continue, not only by condemning discrimination, but above all through an effective and intelligent campaign for the promotion of women.

While much of the debate about the role of women in the Catholic Church has centered on ordination to the priesthood, the Pope argues that he could not change Church teaching—that only men be ordained priests—even if he wanted to. If a priest acts "in the person of Christ" and Christ was a male, the line of priests, at least in the Catholic Church, must continue only among men. No one, man or woman, has the "right" to become a priest. But if Christ chose only men as priests, it was not accidental or because of cultural conditioning, John Paul reasons, and does not detract from the role of women or from others in the Church who are not ordained.

A diversity of roles is in no way prejudicial to women, the Pontiff maintains, as long as it is not an arbitrary imposition, but rather the expression of what is specific to being male and female. Equality does not exclude complementarity, and he sees womanhood expressing all that is human just as much as manhood does, but in a different and complementary way.

John Paul acknowledges the contributions of women in the Church and in the world throughout history. The contributions are all the more notable in light of limited educational opportunities and centuries of bias. He often cites two great women saints in particular, Catherine of Siena and Teresa of Ávila, both of whom have been granted the title of Doctor of the Church. This title has been awarded to only two dozen writers whose tremendous insights have helped develop Church learning. John Paul him-

self declared the French saint, Thérèse of Lisieux, a Doctor of the Church in 1997.

The Pope has denounced the "long and degrading history" of sexual violence against women and the widespread sexist culture that encourages the exploitation of women and even of young girls. Despite some progress, he regrets that "many women have been and continue to be valued more for their physical appearance than for their skill, their professionalism, their intellectual abilities, their deep sensitivity."

Obstacles in many parts of the world keep women marginalized and often subservient. At the same time, certain societies penalize rather than reward motherhood, and in so doing discriminate against those who have chosen to be wives and mothers. Women are better than men at acknowledging people, recognizing their value as individuals, John Paul writes. He believes this may be related to their potential for motherhood, and especially to the period of pregnancy: "This unique contact with the new human being developing within her gives rise to an attitude toward human beings—not only toward her own child, but every human being—which profoundly marks the woman's personality."

I wish to make an appeal on behalf of women whose basic rights are still denied today by the political regimes of their countries: women who are segregated, forbidden to study or to exercise a profession, or even to express their thoughts in public. May international solidarity hasten the due recognition of their rights.

*March 8th Angelus Prayer, Vatican City, 1998*

Respect for the full equality of man and woman in every walk of life is one of civilization's great achievements. Women themselves, with their deeply felt and generous daily witness, have contributed to this, as have the organized movements which, especially in our century, have put this subject before world attention.

*June 25th Angelus Prayer, Vatican City, 1995*

In [Christ's] time women were weighed down by an inherited mentality in which they were deeply discriminated against. The Lord's attitude was a "consistent protest against whatever offends the dignity of women." Indeed, he established a relationship with women which was distinguished by great freedom and friendship.

*June 25th Angelus Prayer, Vatican City, 1995*

*Lomé, Togo, 1985*

How many women have been and are still valued more for their physical appearance than for their personal qualities, professional competence, intellectual work, the richness of their sensitivity and, finally, for the very dignity of their being!

*March 8th Angelus Prayer, Vatican City, 1998*

We can glimpse the characteristic features of the feminine apostolate in our times too: humble initiative, respect for individuals without seeking to impose a way of seeing things, the invitation to repeat the same experience as a way of reaching the same personal conviction of faith.

*July 13th General Audience, Vatican City, 1994*

In the family women have the opportunity and the responsibility to transmit the faith in the early training of their children. They are particularly responsible for the joyful task of leading them to discover the supernatural world.

*July 13th General Audience, Vatican City, 1994*

*Poland, 1979*

gain: woman has an understanding, sensitive and compassionate heart that allows her to give a delicate, concrete style to charity. We know that in the Church there have always been many women— religious and lay, mothers of families and single—who have been dedicated to relieving human suffering.

*July 13th General Audience, Vatican City, 1994*

May Mary, the model of a fulfilled woman, help everyone, especially all women, to understand the "feminine genius," not only to carry out God's precise plan, but also to make more room for women in the various areas of social life.

*March 8th  Angelus Prayer, Vatican City, 1998*

*Icon in the Sanctuary of the Aglona Basilica, Latvia, 1993*

# WORK & REST

hile he is at heart a philosopher and an intellectual, John Paul II spent part of his youth working in a stone quarry and a water-purification plant, and is much more familiar with hard labor than are most priests. He has fond memories of that experience due to the many kindnesses he received from his fellow laborers, who knew he was an underground seminarian. The Nazis, who occupied Poland, had shut down the archdiocesan seminary.

The Pope has reflected at length about what work means for people in his encyclical *Laborem Exercens,* and he also celebrates the world of work each March 19th, the feast of St. Joseph, Christ's foster father and the patron saint of workers. For many years, John Paul visited a different factory on that holiday to spend some time with the employees and reflect on the importance of work.

Justice, the virtue of giving each person his or her due, is essential in the workplace, according to John Paul. When justice is done, workers will strive to become ever more competent at what they do. Organized labor should serve the cause of justice and assure not only that just payment is made for services rendered but also that workers understand both their rights and their duties.

The human person, in his or her dignity as a child of God, always has to be at the center of the workplace, and the Christian vision of work sees it as a way in which a person can develop not only professionally but also spiritually and culturally. Such things as jealousy, power struggles, and unbridled competition—which the Pope points out are all the result of sin—can introduce suffering in one's work experience. A workplace that is centered only on efficiency and profit can also trample on the rights of individuals.

The Pope warns against an exaggerated emphasis on profit, success, and material gains, quoting the words of Jesus in the Gospel of Luke: "For what does it profit a man, if he gain the whole world, but ruin or lose himself?" In a recent Apostolic letter called *Dies Domini* (The Lord's Day), the Pope explains that, over the centuries, the Church has made laws concerning Sunday rest, and "has had in mind above all the work of servants and workers, certainly not because this work was any less worthy when compared to the spiritual requirements of Sunday observance, but rather because it needed greater regulation to lighten its burden and thus enable everyone to keep the Lord's Day holy." John Paul worries particularly about the situation of those Christians who have to make heroic sacrifices to obey the commandment to honor the Lord's Day because they are living in countries in which they are in the minority and Sunday is a workday.

Sunday is above all the day of Our Lord's Resurrection, not simply a day of rest after a hard week of work. Rest is important, for body and soul, but it goes hand in hand with worship, and John Paul asks that Sunday be safeguarded so it can be lived in all its depth. For Catholics, that means time for Mass, which the Pope calls the "heart of Sunday," but also for relaxation with others. Through Sunday rest, daily concerns and tasks can find their proper perspective; he writes: "The material things about which we worry give way to spiritual values; in a moment of encounter and less pressured exchange, we see the true face of the people with whom we live."

*Lorenzago di Cadore, Dolomite Alps, Italy, 1987*

The needs which you are called to answer are numerous. First among them, obviously, is that of promoting employment and fighting unemployment. This latter is always an evil and, when it reaches certain levels, it can become a true social disaster, even more painful when we consider the ominous consequences that it entails for families and young people.

*Address to the National Councils of Labor Consultants of Italy, Spain and Poland, Vatican City, 1998*

What about the work that mothers do at home for their families? Should we not work with greater concern for a legitimate social reevaluation of maternal tasks? I sincerely hope that time is taken to consider these requirements, which have been expressed by many people, giving concrete value to the hard work connected with domestic tasks and the need that children have for the care, love and affection of their parents and especially of their mother.

*Address to the National Councils of Labor Consultants of Italy, Spain and Poland, Vatican City, 1998*

Public authorities must work both directly and indirectly for the achievement of full and dignified employment. . . . According to the principle of solidarity, the weakest must be defended by putting limits on the autonomy of the parties who decide on working conditions, and by always ensuring the basic essentials for the unemployed worker.

*Address to Members of the Regional Board and Council of Lazio, Vatican City, 1998*

*Vatican City, 1988*

I would like to remind everyone that human work contains a "small part of the cross of Christ" and, if accepted with love, has a glimmer of new life, of the new good, as if it were an announcement of "the new heavens and the new earth" in which man and the world participate precisely through the toil that goes with work.

*Audience with Brazilian Bishops, Vatican City, 1995*

We all in fact need an occasional period of extended physical, psychological and spiritual rest. Especially for those who live in large cities, it is important that they immerse themselves in nature for a while. For a vacation to be truly such and bring genuine well-being, in it a person must recover a good balance with himself, with others and with the environment. It is this interior and exterior harmony which revitalizes the mind and reinvigorates body and spirit.

*July 6th Angelus Prayer, Vatican City, 1997*

---

One of the values of a holiday is that of meeting and spending time with others in an unselfish way, for the pleasure of friendship and for sharing quiet moments together.

*July 6th Angelus Prayer, Vatican City, 1997*

*Esch, Luxembourg, 1985*

# II
# The People of God

Christianity can never be reduced to a set of rules and regulations; it is above all a person, Jesus Christ, perfect God and perfect man. It was he who told the Prince of the Apostles, "You are Peter, and upon this rock, I will build my Church, and the gates of hell will not prevail against it." Those are the tremendous claims of Catholicism: that God became man and that he founded his Church on the shoulders of a poor fisherman.

*Caracas, Venezuela, 1985*

ABOVE: *"All Saints before God the Father," from* The Book of Hours of Catherine of Cleves

he Pope's motto, *Totus Tuus,* says everything about his devotion to the Virgin Mary. The Latin words, meaning "all yours," are the beginning of a Latin prayer composed by a French saint, Louis-Marie Grignion de Montfort. This motto and the M on John Paul II's coat of arms both refer to Mary. He chose these some 20 years before he was made a successor of St. Peter, when he was named bishop in Poland.

John Paul again professed his love for and total trust in the Madonna on the very night he was elected. And since then, nearly every major document the Pope has written or speech he has given has concluded with an appeal for the intercession of the Mother of God. Just hours after his fellow cardinals chose him as Pope in October 1978, John Paul acknowledged that he was afraid to accept the task he had been given. "But I did it in the spirit of obedience to our Lord Jesus Christ and of total confidence in his Mother, the most holy Madonna. I present myself to you all to confess our common faith, our hope, our confidence

in the Mother of Christ and of the Church."

In the story of his own priestly vocation, *Gift and Mystery,* the Pope credits Grignion de Montfort with clarifying for him the answer to a question many Christians ask themselves: What is the proper role of Mary in my life? Protestants have often criticized Catholics for "worshiping" Mary; the Church responds that worship is due to God alone, but Mary deserves special attention as the Mother of Jesus Christ. She is the greatest of saints, since she was born without sin, but she is still a creature, meaning she is less than God because she was created by God.

The Pope recalled that as a young priest he began to question his devotion to Mary, since he was worried that if it became too great, it might end up somehow weakening the worship due to Christ. (This is exactly the Protestant critique of the role of Mary in Catholic theology.) But Grignion de Montfort's book, *Treatise of True Devotion to the Blessed Virgin,* helped him see that Mary brings a believer closer to Christ.

The future Pope also discovered the

importance of the words of the Angelus prayer, the same one he recites every Sunday at noon and on feast days with the pilgrims in St. Peter's Square: "The Angel of the Lord declared unto Mary and she conceived of the Holy Spirit. . . . Behold the handmaid of the Lord. . . . Be it done unto me according to your word. . . . And the word became flesh and dwelt among us." They are the words that describe what John Paul considers the greatest event in all of history, the Incarnation, or God becoming man.

The Pope's Marian devotion rests on that event, on this woman's role in the history of salvation. Mary was free to say no when as a young girl she was startled by the visit of the Archangel Gabriel, who revealed God's plan for her. John Paul believes that never in history has so much depended on the free cooperation of one of God's creatures.

His devotion to Mary began at an early age, with visits to the image of Our Lady of Perpetual Help in his parish church in Wadowice. Later, when he was studying in Kraków, he would frequently visit a church that had a particular devotion to Mary, Help of Christians. As a priest and bishop, he would also make many pilgrimages to Kalwaria Zebrzydowska, the main Marian shrine in the Archdiocese of Kraków. He would walk along the paths there and pray for the Church during the difficult years of Communist rule in Poland.

Those Marian visits have now extended well beyond Poland and brought him to all the major Marian shrines around the world, from Lourdes in France and Fatima in Portugal to Guadalupe in Mexico and dozens of other smaller shrines as far away as Japan. But above all has been a constant recourse to Mary, almost like a small child pestering his mother for help. Mariologists, or those who study the Blessed Virgin Mary, believe that no Pope has ever emphasized the significance of Mary as has John Paul.

When he was in Kraków in 1976, Cardinal Wojtyla was called to Rome by Pope Paul VI to preach the annual Lenten retreat to top Vatican officials. Following tradition, Paul VI attended that retreat, and so it was a great honor for Wojtyla to lead it. What the then-cardinal said about Mary was noteworthy:

"Both holy scripture . . . and the experience of the faithful see the Mother of God as the one who, in a very special way, is united with the Church at the most difficult moments in her history, when the attacks on her become most threatening."

Those looked like prophetic words just five years later, when John Paul was shot and nearly killed in St. Peter's Square. The date was May 13, 1981, the day of the feast of Our Lady of Fatima. The Pope believes it was Mary who miraculously saved his life, and he later placed one of the bullets that hit him in the crown of the statue of Our Lady of Fatima in Portugal.

*Garden at Castel Gondolfo, near Rome, 1985*

*Our Lady of Czestochowa, also known as the Black Madonna, Czestochowa, Poland. This icon is held especially dear in the hearts of many Polish people. Each year many hundreds of thousands of people make the pilgrimage to see the Madonna in the Czestochowa Basilica.*

The special gifts which God had showered on Mary made her particularly suited to her task as mother and teacher. In the concrete circumstances of everyday life, Jesus could find in her a model to follow and imitate and an example of perfect love for God and for his brothers and sisters.

*December 4th General Audience, Vatican City, 1996*

Although occurring by the work of the Holy Spirit and a Virgin Mother, the birth of Jesus, like that of all human beings, went through the phases of conception, gestation and delivery. In addition, Mary's motherhood was not limited to the biological process of giving birth, but as it happens with every other mother, she also made an essential contribution to her Son's growth and development.

A mother is not only a woman who gives birth to a child, but one who brings him up and teaches him; indeed, we might well say that, according to God's plan, the educational task is the natural extension of procreation.

*December 4th General Audience, Vatican City, 1996*

To the Blessed Virgin, *tota pulchra*, all beautiful, we entrust our resolutions. May Mary obtain for us the courage not to give in to our frailty, in the awareness that God's love is greater than sin. The Lord, who in Mary did great things, will also be able to accomplish wonderful things in those who sincerely accept his invitation to conversion and love.

*December 8th Angelus Prayer, Vatican City, 1996*

*Lourdes, 1983*

May the Blessed Virgin help us to make her Son's new life our own, by accepting the gift of divine mercy which enables us to be artisans of forgiveness, reconciliation and peace. May she inspire in all who have governmental responsibilities at the national and international level the necessary courage to intervene promptly and wisely in difficult situations before they become irreparable and more blood is shed in vain.

*Regina Caeli Prayer, Vatican City, 1997*

Of course, the Blessed Virgin is totally related to Christ, the foundation of faith and ecclesial experience, and she leads to him. That is why, in obedience to Jesus, who reserved a very special role for his Mother in the economy of salvation, Christians have venerated, loved and prayed to Mary in a most particular and fervent way. They have attributed to her an important place in faith and piety, recognizing her as the privileged way to Christ, the supreme Mediator.

*November 15th General Audience, Vatican City, 1995*

*This facsimile of the Our Lady of Czestochowa icon was one of the many such reproductions distributed to parishes throughout Poland as a symbol of national pride during the grassroots struggle against Communism in the eighties. Kraków, 1983.*

Like Mary, you must not be afraid to allow the Holy Spirit to help you become intimate friends of Christ. Like Mary, you must put aside any fear, in order to take Christ to the world in whatever you do—in marriage, as single people in the world, as students, as workers, as professional people. Christ wants to go to many places in the world, and to enter many hearts, through you.

*Homily, New York, 1995*

Uniting ourselves with Mary, a pilgrim in the faith, we are strengthened in the conviction that every second of life is a precious moment of grace that teaches us to welcome Christ as our sure hope.

*Homily, Message for World Day of the Sick, Vatican City, 1994*

This woman of faith, Mary of Nazareth, the Mother of God, has been given to us as a model in our pilgrimage of faith. From Mary we learn to surrender to God's will in all things. From Mary, we learn to trust even when all hope seems gone. From Mary, we learn to love Christ, her Son and the Son of God. For Mary is not only the Mother of God, she is Mother of the Church as well.

*Message to Priests, Washington, D.C., 1979*

*Fatima, Portugal, 1982*

# VOCATION

or the Pope, the special call to serve God—what he calls the grandeur of a vocation—means loving Christ above all else as a way to freedom and happiness. Blessed are those men and women who have been attracted by the power of the word of God and molded by the sacraments: "They are setting out on the path of total and radical belonging to God, strengthened by the hope that does not disappoint." The Church needs modern-day apostles, and the Holy Spirit continues to call them, John Paul II says. To encourage those who are hesitant to leave everything to follow Christ, he has often referred to his own joy and security when he realized that God wanted him to become a priest.

There are frequent debates about a recent "vocations crisis" in the Catholic Church, but if it is a crisis, it is one that has been going on for a long time—for centuries, in fact. Christ himself had observed, "The harvest is plentiful, but the laborers are few." John Paul acknowledges there is a problem of vocations, which affects not only individual religious orders and countries that do not have enough priests, but the entire Church.

The sacraments are essential to the Catholic faith, and some require ordination to be administered. Only a priest can celebrate the Eucharist, hear confessions, and anoint the sick. "The whole people of God rejoices when young men are willing to prepare themselves for the priesthood, which is indispensable for the Church's growth and sanctification," John Paul writes. In areas in which there are not a sufficient number of priests, especially in Africa and Latin America, some communities go without the regular celebration of Sunday Mass and other sacraments. In these cases, John Paul calls on all Catholics to raise a "fervent prayer to the Lord of the harvest for an increase of vocations."

Although the number of vocations to the priesthood has increased under his pontificate, many areas of the world still feel an acute crisis. Many progressive-minded Catholics believe that opening up the priesthood to single women and to married people of both sexes would improve the situation. But John Paul has been a staunch opponent of both ideas. If Christ himself did not choose women when he instituted the priesthood, there cannot be women priests today, he argues. And although married priests are permitted in many other denominations, including the Church of England and all Orthodox Churches, the Pope sees celibacy as a manifestation of one's willingness to follow Christ in complete dedication.

However, John Paul has made it a point to commend women religious who have served society with exemplary generosity, especially in the fields of education and health care. Also, he never fails to note how cloistered nuns have made a total self-offering to God by dedicating their lives to prayer. These, among others, are the indispensable positions that women fulfill within the Church.

Despite a lack of priests in many parts of the world, John Paul has repeatedly told bishops to be sure to select their seminarians well; that not everyone is fit to be a priest. He is concerned that seminarians be mature, well-balanced, and prayerful men who have the right intentions. John Paul reminds them that their vocation is not one of honor or power, but of service to God and to the faithful. On several occasions, the Pope has spoken about the "radical" choice to become a priest or a female or male member of a religious order: "While they are necessary in every age, these vocations are even more necessary today, in a world marked by great contradictions and the temptation to relegate God to the margins in the fundamental choices of life."

OVERLEAF: *College of Cardinals, Vatican City, 1985*

It is also important to take into account that the vocations apostolate begins with and finds its context in the pastoral care of youth, directed to the doctrinal, spiritual and apostolic care of young people, both in parishes and schools and in the movements and activities outside the parish.

*Address to Argentine Bishops, Vatican City, 1995*

If bishops and priests are to be truly effective witnesses to Christ and teachers of the faith, they have to be men of prayer like Christ himself.

*Address to U.S. Bishops, Vatican City, 1998*

Christ is knocking very hard at many hearts, looking for young people like you to send into the vineyard where an abundant harvest is ready.

*Address on World Youth Day, Denver, Colorado, 1993*

The parish is a "family of families" and should be organized to support family life in every way possible. . . . Priests are called to a unique form of spiritual fatherhood and can come to a deeper appreciation of the meaning of being a "man for others" through their pastoral care of those striving to live out the requirements of self-giving and fruitful love in Christian marriage.

*Address to U.S. Bishops, Vatican City, 1998*

*Vienna, 1983*

We need many priests, but we want them to be suitable, worthy, well-prepared and holy.

*Address to Argentine Bishops, Vatican City, 1995*

*Ordination of new priests, St. Peter's Basilica, Vatican City, 1980*

OVERLEAF: *Seville, Spain, 1982*

*St. Peter's Square, Vatican City, 1985*

**P**riests are the special witnesses and ministers of God's mercy. At no other time can they be as close to the faithful as when they lead them to the crucified and forgiving Christ in this uniquely personal encounter. To be the minister of the sacrament of Reconciliation is a special privilege for a priest who, acting in the person of Christ, is permitted to enter into the drama of another Christian life in a singular way.

*Address to U.S. Bishops, Vatican City, 1998*

*Kottayam, India, 1986*

OVERLEAF: *Nagasaki, Japan, 1981*

# SAINTS

ope John Paul II believes in miracles, God's intervening in extraordinary ways in the lives of men, women, and children. He also believes in the intercession of the saints and other holy people who can successfully pray to God for his divine intervention.

When he was Archbishop of Kraków, in 1962, Karol Wojtyla wrote a letter to an Italian monk, Padre Pio of Pietrelcina, who was reputed to be a very holy man, with special powers before God. The archbishop's letter—written in Latin—explained to the simple priest that a woman he knew, the mother of four daughters, was suffering from cancer, and he asked him to pray for her cure. On seeing the letter, Padre Pio reportedly said, "To this request I cannot say no." God apparently could not say no, either, and four days later the woman, Wanda Poltawska, was cured. In May 1999, John Paul had the joy of putting Padre Pio on the first step of official sainthood in the Catholic Church by declaring him "blessed."

After beatification, one becomes eligible for canonization, or the declaration of sainthood. Martyrdom is sufficient for

someone to be declared blessed, but to be made a saint, at least one miracle is necessary. For those who were not martyred, two miracles—usually cures that are medically inexplicable—have to be verified by physicians.

All of the Apostles, with the exception of Judas Iscariot, are venerated as saints, as are the founders of the major religious orders, such as St. Benedict, St. Francis, and St. Dominic. Saints have changed the face of the Church and the world. St. Catherine of Siena, for example, helped persuade Pope Gregory XI to return to Rome from Avignon in the 14th century, while in the 16th century St. Francis Xavier brought the message of Christ halfway around the world, to India and Japan. Some of the Pope's favorite saints include the Spanish mystic St. John of the Cross and St. Jean-Baptiste-Marie Vianney, better known as the Curé of Ars—a simple and austere French priest who spent much of his life hearing confessions and offering sacrifices for the conversion of souls.

Although some of the candidates for holiness are known for their supernatural powers—Padre Pio could reportedly foretell the future, for example—others led more ordinary lives. Miracles are necessary for sainthood, but the most important aspect in the life of a saint is that he or she has lived the Christian virtues—justice, prudence, fortitude, temperance, faith, hope, charity—to a heroic degree. Virtue requires considerable effort, and heroic virtue requires heroic effort, but John Paul wants to show that it can be achieved in any place and under any circumstances. He has special affection for Mother Teresa and her work with the poorest of the poor. Although she has not yet been declared blessed, the process has begun.

John Paul sees conferring sainthood as a way of showing the faithful that a life of Christian heroism is possible. The beatifications and canonizations of John Paul have far outnumbered those of all his predecessors in this century. After 21 years on the throne of St. Peter, he has beatified more than 900 people and canonized more than 280.

The great majority of both of those groups are martyrs, those who gave their lives for the faith. It was precisely the blood of the martyrs that sparked devotion to the saints in the early Church. Faithful pilgrims would visit the martyrs' tombs on a regular basis, knowing that because of the martyrs' generous sacrifice, they now found favor with God. The site of St. Peter's Basilica in Rome was specifically chosen because it was the place where Peter, the Prince of the Apostles, was martyred and buried.

At the end of the second millennium, the Church has once again become a Church of martyrs. Recent persecution against Christians has led to the deaths of priests, nuns, and laypeople in countries all over the world, from Uganda to Japan, and the Pope does not want that witness to be lost. He has been particularly keen to honor the Catholic victims of the Nazis in World War II, and those people—especially nuns and priests—who were murdered by Communists and anarchists during the Spanish Civil War.

Most of the individuals canonized or beatified by John Paul have been celebrated by vast groups of people, not only Catholics. An official declaration of holiness tends to bring people together, especially in countries in which there is no history of Catholic saints. When the Pope declares someone blessed in Australia or Papua New Guinea or Nigeria, it is cause for national celebration and newfound pride in a native son or daughter. It also demonstrates the Catholic Church's universality, its role as a Church for all peoples and nations.

On the threshold of the third millennium, we are encouraged to read the signs of the time more attentively. We stand before the ecumenism of the martyrs and saints, the witness, that is, of so many sons and daughters of the various Churches and ecclesial communities whose example is already the common heritage of all Christians.

*Address to the Bulgarian Delegation, Vatican City, 1995*

Love of God then is the source of true joy. This is what our brothers and sisters in faith personally experienced. They are presented to the Church today as models of generous adherence to the Lord's commandment. They are blessed. In their earthly lives, they lived the love of God in a very special way and for this reason, they were able to delight in the fullness of joy promised by Christ. Today they are held up for our veneration as privileged witnesses to the love of God. By their example and intercession they show the way to that complete happiness which is the profound aspiration of the human soul.

*Homily at the Beatification of Five Blesseds, Vatican City, 1997*

*A portrait of St. Maximilian Kolbe in the Citadel of the Immaculate, which Kolbe founded in Nagasaki, Japan. Kolbe was canonized in 1982. This picture was taken in 1981.*

The example of people who live holy lives teaches us not only to practice mutual respect and understanding, but to be ourselves models of goodness, reconciliation and collaboration, across ethnic and religious boundaries, for the good of the whole country and for the greater glory of God.

*Meeting with Muslim leaders, Abuja, Nigeria, 1998*

God calls everyone to holiness, but without forcing anyone's hand. God asks and waits for man's free acceptance. In the context of this universal call to holiness, Christ then chooses a specific task for each person and if he finds a response, he himself provides for bringing the work he has begun to completion, ensuring that the fruit remains.

*Homily at the Beatification of Five Blesseds, Vatican City, 1997*

In communion with the particular Churches where they lived and worked, let us offer our praise to the Lord for the marvels worked by his grace in our glorious brothers and sisters in the faith. At the same time, we feel encouraged by them to become ever more convinced witnesses of Christ the Lord, to proclaim him with our words and our life. May the spiritual closeness and fraternal support of their powerful intercession comfort us.

*Audience with a Pilgrim Group at the Beatification of Five Blesseds, Vatican City, 1997*

*The Pope in front of a portrait of St. Teresa of Ávila, Ávila, Spain, 1982*

OVERLEAF: *With Mother Teresa, Albania, 1993*

hen one close adviser to John Paul II was asked how the Pope made decisions, the response was, "On his knees." He was not joking, either. John Paul truly believes in the power of prayer. Sometimes he will prostrate himself before the altar, in total submission to God's will. He believes prayer can work miracles, large and small. He prays not only for the "big intentions," like achieving peace in the world and helping people discover Christ, but also for the requests that the faithful send him. In his kneeler at the front of his private chapel is a big stack of yellow sheets, each with eight or ten names on it, most of them those of sick people in countries around the world.

The Pope recalls that after his mother's death, when he was only eight, his father's life became one of continual prayer. Young Karol would sometimes wake at night and see his father on his knees in prayer, just as he would often see him kneeling in the local parish church. The Pontiff has followed that example quite closely, and spends an hour each morning in prayer in his private chapel before celebrating Mass. Until he broke his leg in 1994, he would spend that time kneeling before the tabernacle and a painting of Our Lady of Czestochowa. Now he remains seated as he carries on his conversation with God.

Nor is morning the only time the Pope prays. From the cupola of St. Peter's Basilica, he can often be glimpsed meditating as he walks the small patio of his Vatican apartment. And, like all priests, he recites the Liturgy of the Hours, the official cycle of the Church's daily prayer at different times during the day. His Marian devotion is expressed in part by praying several meditations on rosaries every day. Each rosary consists of five mysteries in the life of Christ or Mary, and ten Hail Marys are recited for each mystery. Some of the mysteries are joyful (the Annunciation, the Visitation, the Nativity, the Presentation of Jesus, and the Finding of the Child Jesus in the Temple). There are also sorrowful mysteries (the Agony in the Garden, the Scourging at the Pillar, the Crowning with Thorns, the Carrying of the Cross, and the Crucifixion). And then there are the glorious mysteries (the Resurrection, the Ascension, the Descent of the Holy Spirit, the Assumption, and the Coronation of the Blessed Virgin).

One of the chief reasons why John Paul has always loved being in the mountains is that nature gives him a chance to meditate on the wonders of creation and to speak with God. Tadeusz Styczen, a close friend of the Pope and a fellow philosopher, recalls that when they used to go skiing together years ago in Poland, Archbishop Wojtyla would often choose to walk up the mountain, skis on his shoulders, rather than take the ski lift. He would do so in almost total silence, in contemplation. John Paul sees a spiritual significance in times of rest. For him, holidays and vacations are not simply an opportunity to escape; they must have a deeper meaning. Men and women, he believes, need to discover the beauty of silence so they can learn how to contemplate, recognizing God's traces in nature and in other human beings.

While he often goes to the mountains to relax and pray, John Paul also speaks of the need to create "desert" spaces within us and around us, what he calls "opportunities to give up what is superfluous, to seek the essential, an atmosphere of silence and prayer." At times, the beauty of nature helps the Pope pray, but on most days he spends hours in front of the tabernacle in which the Holy Eucharist is reserved. He has asked that Eucharistic adoration be a regular practice in all parishes and Christian communities, because he believes that even the most serious problems can be resolved in the presence of the Blessed Sacrament. For the Pope, the ideal place to pray is before the tabernacle.

In his book *Crossing the Threshold of Hope,* the Pope describes prayer as a conversation, but one in which the "you" is much more important than the "I," since prayer begins with God. The true protagonists in prayer are God the Father, the Son, and the Holy Spirit. He writes: "Man achieves the fullness of prayer not when he expresses himself, but when he lets God be most fully present in prayer." Talking with God does not mean trying to change God's will but making ourselves properly disposed to accept that will, even if doing so requires sacrifices on our part.

John Paul believes that Mary represents the model of prayer for Christians, because of her total willingness to do whatever God wanted of her. That is prayer in its essence: discovering God's will and then trying to carry it out. As the Holy Father told an audience gathered at St. Peter's in 1997: "Her example shows us that worship does not primarily consist in expressing human thoughts and feelings, but in listening to the divine word in order to know it, assimilate it, and put it into practice in daily life."

OVERLEAF: *Valle d'Aosta, Italy, 1989*

**Y**es, God alone is our true and unfailing support, just as love and prayer are the only sure spiritual levers with which it is possible to lift up the world. And this applies to all areas of life.

*November 6th Angelus Prayer, Siracusa, Sicily, 1994*

**O**ur true mother tongue is the praise of God, the language of heaven, our true home. . . . As we look at the century we are leaving behind, we see that human pride and sin have made it difficult for many people to speak their mother tongue. In order to be able to sing God's praises we must relearn the language of humility and trust, the language of moral integrity and of sincere commitment to all that is truly good in the sight of the Lord.

*Celebration of Evening Prayer in St. Louis, Missouri, 1999*

**T**oday we are living in an age of instant communications. But do you realize what a unique form of communication prayer is? Prayer enables us to meet God at the most profound level of our being. It connects us directly to God, the living God: Father, Son and Holy Spirit, in a constant exchange of love.

*Discourse to Youth, St. Louis, Missouri, 1999*

*The Pope's private chapel, Vatican City, 1986*

**O**nly the human person, created in the image and likeness of God, is capable of raising a hymn of praise and thanksgiving to the Creator. The earth, with all its creatures, and the entire universe call on man to be their voice.

*Homily, San Antonio, Texas, 1987*

**P**rayer joined to sacrifice constitutes the most powerful force in human history.

*January 12th General Audience, Vatican City, 1994*

**P**rayer can truly change your life. For it turns your attention away from yourself and directs your mind and your heart toward the Lord. If we look only at ourselves, with our limitations and sins, we quickly give way to sadness and discouragement. But if we keep our eyes fixed on the Lord, then our hearts are filled with hope, our minds are washed in the light of truth, and we come to know the fullness of the Gospel with all its promise and life.

*Meeting with Youth, New Orleans, Louisiana, 1987*

*Nuoro, Sardinia, 1985*

OVERLEAF: *Piazza di Spagna, Rome, 1983*

# FORGIVENESS

rom the very begin-
ning of his pontificate,
John Paul II has been
preparing for the
Jubilee Year, the two
thousandth anniver-
sary of the birth of Christ and a time for
great celebration. For the Pope, the
Jubilee is above all about the "joy of
forgiveness." All of God's children have a
tendency to stray from their true home,
and a jubilee—which in the time of the
Old Testament was a time for slaves to be
freed and debts to be canceled—marks a
perfect time to return home. The Pope
calls on the faithful to convert and change
their lives—to make them more centered
on God and less on worldly concerns.

"Let no one in this Jubilee Year wish
to exclude himself from the Father's
embrace," the Pope writes as he compares
the life of every Christian to that of the
prodigal son in the Gospel, who squan-
ders the riches his father has left him. But
the father, who represents God the
Father, loves his son dearly and anxiously
awaits the young man's return from loose
living and squalor, which represent the
misery of sin. The Gospel story describes
in detail the joy of the father, who sees his
son coming from afar. He embraces the
young man and tells his servants to pre-

pare the fatted calf, music, and a wonderful feast to celebrate his son's return.
Although the parable is known as that of
the "prodigal son," it could just as easily
be called that of the "merciful father."

In the parable, there is also the
"good" older brother, the one who never
went astray yet stubbornly resists joining
the party despite his father's pleadings.
"Let no one behave like the elder brother
in the Gospel parable who refuses to
enter the house to celebrate," the Pope
writes. "May the joy of forgiveness be
stronger and greater than any resent-
ment." Concretely, the Pontiff recom-
mends that for the Jubilee all Catholics
make a full examination of conscience
and a complete confession, asking forgiveness for their sins from a Father who
is kind and full of mercy.

John Paul surprised a number of people when he asked that the entire Church
make an examination of conscience for all
those times in history when Christians
"departed from the spirit of Christ and
his Gospel." It marked a clear shift away
from the arrogance with which the faith
was sometimes defended in the past. The
Pontiff exhorted Catholics to prepare for
the year 2000 with a clear awareness of
the events of the last two thousand years.
The Church has nothing to fear by

admitting sins of the past, he argued: "She cannot cross the threshold of the new millennium without encouraging her children to purify themselves, through repentance, of past errors and instances of infidelity, inconsistency and slowness to act. Acknowledging the weaknesses of the past is an act of honesty and courage that helps us to strengthen our faith."

The Pope did not mention any specific events, but referred indirectly to wars of religion and the execution of heretics. "Another painful chapter of history to which the sons and daughters of the Church must return with a spirit of repentance is that of the acquiescence given, especially in certain centuries, to intolerance and even to the use of violence in the service of truth." John Paul said the cultural conditioning of the times and other historical factors had to be taken into account, but that the darker moments of the Church's history could not be whitewashed. "The consideration of mitigating factors does not exonerate the Church from the obligation to express profound regret for the weaknesses of so many of her sons and daughters who sullied her face."

In his 1997 *Message for Peace*, "Offer Forgiveness and Receive Peace," the Pope said that offering and accepting forgiveness are essential conditions for authentic peace. He admits that forgiveness—either asking for it or granting it—can seem contrary to human instinct, in which revenge often prevails: "But forgiveness is inspired by the logic of love, that love which God has for every man and woman, for every people and nation, and for the whole human family." If the Church dares proclaim what from a human standpoint might appear to be sheer folly, it is because of her confidence in God's infinite love and mercy.

For John Paul, both asking and granting forgiveness spring from the recognition that we are all sinners. Most of the great saints were men and women who often got down on their knees to confess their sins, and the Pope has encouraged the ordinary faithful to do the same. Every Good Friday, he spends some time in the confessional himself, hearing the confessions of visitors to St. Peter's Basilica. His most striking gesture of forgiveness, however, remains his 1983 visit to the gunman who had tried to kill him two and a half years before. Even from his hospital bed, just four days after the shooting, with a weak voice John Paul asked for prayers "for the brother who shot me and whom I have sincerely forgiven."

Confession is an act of honesty and courage; an act of entrusting ourselves, beyond sin, to the mercy of a loving and forgiving God. It is an act of the prodigal son who returns to his father and is welcomed by him with the kiss of peace.

*Homily, San Antonio, Texas, 1987*

When we realize that God's love for us does not cease in the face of our sin or recoil before our offenses, but becomes even more attentive and generous; when we realize that this love went so far as to cause the passion and death of the word made flesh who consented to redeem us at the price of his own blood, then we exclaim in gratitude: "Yes, the Lord is rich in mercy," and even: "The Lord is mercy."

*Reconciliatio et Paenitentia (Reconciliation and Penance in the Mission of the Church Today), Vatican City, 1984*

*A gun is raised above the crowd, St. Peter's Square, Vatican City, May 13, 1981*

*The Pope is shot, St. Peter's Square, Vatican City, May 13, 1981*

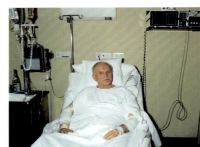

*Policlinico Gemelli, Rome, 1981*

*A conversation with Ali Agca, the Pope's attacker, in the Rebibbia jail, Rome, December 27, 1983*

Forgiveness demonstrates the presence in the world of the love which is more powerful than sin. Forgiveness is also the fundamental condition for reconciliation, not only in the relationship of God with man, but also in relationships between people. A world from which forgiveness was eliminated would be nothing but a world of cold and unfeeling justice, in the name of which each person would claim his or her own rights vis-à-vis others.

*Dives in Misericordia (Rich in Mercy), Vatican City, 1980*

To cut oneself off from Penance is to cut oneself off from an irreplaceable form of encounter with Christ. So, priests themselves should receive this sacrament regularly and in a spirit of genuine faith and devotion. In this way, the priest's own constant conversion to the Lord is strengthened, and the faithful see more clearly that reconciliation with God and the Church is necessary for authentic Christian living.

*Address to U.S. Bishops, Vatican City, 1998*

*The Pope hears confession, St. Peter's Basilica, Vatican City, 1986*

It must be emphasized that the most precious result of the forgiveness obtained in the sacrament of Penance consists in reconciliation with God, which takes place in the inmost heart of the son who was lost and found again, which every penitent is. But it has to be added that this reconciliation with God leads, as it were, to other reconciliations which repair the breaches caused by sin. The forgiven penitent is reconciled with himself in his inmost being, where he regains his own true identity. He is reconciled with his brethren whom he has in some way attacked and wounded. He is reconciled with the Church. He is reconciled with all creation.

*Reconciliatio et Paenitentia (Reconciliation and Penance in the Mission of the Church Today), Vatican City, 1984*

*Wall of Death, Auschwitz, 1979*

# DEATH & ETERNAL LIFE

uman history, John Paul II believes, is marked by a frantic and tragic search for something or someone who can free humanity from death and guarantee life. The human heart wants to be happy, and not only momentarily; it is looking for joy without end. While everyone has moments of crisis and weariness, despondency and gloom, Christ came to provide the ultimate answer to each person's yearning for life and for the infinite. Jesus Christ is the Lord of life, the author and the source of life without end. When speaking to young people, the Pope often quotes Christ's words from the Gospel of St. John: "I am the Way, and the Truth and the Life." Christ, perfect God and perfect man, came to earth to show men and women the path to immortality, to make it accessible to them.

Among the first words that John Paul pronounced upon his election were, "Be not afraid!" and he has repeated this gentle admonition on numerous occasions in the course of his pontificate. They are the words of Christ himself to the Apostles. We should fear neither God's mystery nor his love. John Paul laments the fact that so many people appear to go through this life unaware that their real goal is eternal life and eternal happiness. Some, the Pontiff remarks, seek their happiness in what is ephemeral, including what he calls the "artificial paradise" of drug abuse. "There are also those who teach that the meaning of life lies solely in the quest for success, the accumulation of wealth, the development of personal abilities, without regard for the needs of others or respect for values," he said in a message to young people in 1992. "These and other kinds of false teachers of life . . . propose goals that not only fail to bring satisfaction but often intensify and exacerbate the thirst that burns in the human heart."

The Pontiff promises that Christ's light, the one that once shone on Bethlehem, illuminates the way of life for all humanity and goes beyond the boundaries of earthly existence, encouraging Christians to walk in the light of faith. The hope of eternal life, the hope of happiness forever, should instill in everyone the necessary courage to face the difficulties of daily life. John Paul points to Psalm 26 as a good prayer for hope in the hereafter: "One thing have I asked of the Lord, that will I seek after; that I may dwell in the house of the Lord all the days of my life."

The same psalm rejoices with hope: "I believe that I shall see the goodness of the Lord in the land of the living!" And yet, John Paul reflects, our daily experience tells us that life is marked by sin and threatened by death, despite the desire for good that beats in our hearts and the desire for life that courses through our veins. Death, in Christian teaching, came as a result of original sin. Yet Christ, in the mystery of his cross and resurrection, has destroyed death and sin. With Christ redeeming man through his crucifixion, the gates of heaven were opened, and man became capable of achieving the glory of eternal life. "O death, where is thy victory?" asks St. Paul. "O death, where is thy sting?"

A truly Christian vision of death does not deny the suffering and anguish that it can bring, as Christ's own death did for Mary and the Apostles. However, it sees death as the door that opens to eternal life, what John Paul has labeled "the true horizon of every human heart." He warns against "too earthly" an interpretation of life, and calls on the faithful to place God at the very center of their existence. The simple phrase "Thy kingdom come" in the "Our Father" is a reminder that one's days on earth must be marked by the daily search for the kingdom of God above everything else.

That kingdom, according to John Paul, has been presented symbolically as "a great and joyful banquet offered to all." Although all are invited to the heavenly feast, not everyone will choose to partake. Some will suffer the torments of hell, and God will be the judge. John Paul believes, however, that "Christ is a divine judge with a human heart, a judge who wants to give life." For a Christian, attaining the glory of heaven, where "every tear shall be wiped away," is worth any and all sacrifices. Death marks the beginning of a new life, one that lasts forever and gives infinite happiness.

*With Mother Teresa at her Nirmal Hriday Ashram, the House of the Pure Heart, Calcutta, 1986*

God's merciful love regenerates every human being; it is by accepting the gift of mercy from the risen Lord that we can build a reconciled world, truly open to the horizons of life, of full and deep joy in the Triune God. After Easter, man is no longer a being for death, but a being for life. The abyss of death has been destroyed by the risen Christ's explosion of life.

*Regina Caeli Prayer, Vatican City, 1997*

The certainty that life continues in a different way from what our eyes behold brings believers to cemeteries. To stand at the graves of one's own loved ones is an occasion for families to reflect on and to nurture their hope in eternity.

*November 2nd General Audience for All Souls Day, Vatican City, 1994*

DEATH & ETERNAL LIFE

**h**owever, he [man] also experiences the irrepressible desire for immortal life. For this reason the bonds of love uniting parents and children, husbands and wives, brothers and sisters, as well as the ties of true friendship between individuals, are not lost nor do they end with the inescapable event of death. Our departed ones continue to live among us, not only because their mortal remains rest in the cemetery and their memory is part of our lives, but especially because their souls intercede for us with God.

*November 2nd General Audience for All Souls Day, Vatican City, 1994*

*Basilica of St. John Lateran, the Pope's seat as bishop of Rome, 1985*

Christ is the King of love and therefore the final judgment on man and his world will be a judgment on love. Our place on one side or the other will depend on whether or not we have loved. The kingdom Christ offers us is also a task given to each of us. It is our responsibility to bring it about through those acts of love described with great realism by the Gospel.

*Homily for the Feast of Christ the King, Vatican City, 1996*

This relationship is spiritual and consists of feelings, memories and especially prayer, which is solidly based on the certainty, already grasped in some way by reason and corroborated by faith, that human life does not end on earth. Death opens to souls a new horizon of life, in the direction marked by God's judgment on the good or evil they have done.

*November 1st Angelus Prayer for All Saints Day, Vatican City, 1994*

We all have our personal history and an innate desire to see God, a desire which makes itself felt at the same time as we discover the created world. This world is wonderful and rich; it sets before us countless treasures; it enchants us; it attracts both our reason and our will. But in the end it does not satisfy our spirit. Man realizes that this world, with all its many riches, is superficial and precarious; in a sense, it is destined for death.

*Message on World Youth Day, Paris, 1997*

*Clonmacnoise, Ireland, 1979*

n the surface, the Pope's ardent desire to see the unity of all Christian denominations seems like nothing more than a dream. Bitter differences between Catholic and Orthodox Christians persist in many parts of Eastern Europe. And, from the Catholic standpoint, the Anglican Church's decision to ordain women was a serious setback to the cause of ecumenism—the effort to bring Christian churches back together. Yet John Paul II believes that God wants Christian unity and that Christ's prayer on the eve of his crucifixion—"that all may be one"—has to be answered.

All the Lord's disciples "are invited by the ever-fresh power of the Gospel to acknowledge with sincere and total objectivity the mistakes made . . . at the origins of their deplorable divisions," the Pontiff writes. "What is needed is a calm, clear-sighted and truthful vision of things, a vision enlivened by divine mercy and capable of freeing people's minds." He recognizes mistakes made on all sides and calls for a change of heart, an interior conversion.

Despite the many sins that have contributed to historical divisions among Christians, John Paul remains convinced that "we are on the way toward full unity." He notes that the very expression "separated brethren," often used in the past, has come to be replaced by expressions that suggest greater unity, such as "other Christians" or "Christians of other communities." All Christians, he states bluntly, belong to Christ and are working toward the same goal, that of proclaiming the Gospel to the men and women of every people and nation.

The Pontiff wants especially to explore the possibilities of union with the Orthodox Church, for whom the supreme authority of the Pope presents a major obstacle. The churches split nearly a thousand years ago, in 1054, but they share the same sacramental system and agree on nearly all points of doctrine. The Pope compares the two churches to the Apostles Peter and Paul, who came from quite different backgrounds—one a poor fisherman and the other a Pharisee and a Roman citizen—and had very diverse spiritual histories. "And yet, despite their different paths and at times their stark contrasts," John Paul argues, "their ambition was the same: to please the Lord. Their origins divide them; their mission unites them."

John Paul has also striven to maintain good relations with the other two great monotheistic religions, Judaism and Islam. A 1985 talk to young people in Casablanca, Morocco, has proved to be the blueprint for what the Pope thinks about living in peace and reciprocal respect with Muslims. The Pontiff spoke of Morocco's long tradition of tolerance and respect, and of the fact that there have always been Jews living in the country, and nearly always Christians.

"Christians and Muslims must recognize with joy the religious values that we have in common, and give thanks to God for it," John Paul said. "Both of us believe in one God, the only God, who is all Justice and all Mercy; we believe in the importance of prayer, of fasting, of alms-giving, of repentance, and of pardon; we believe that God will be a merciful judge to us at the end of time, and we hope that after the Resurrection he will be satisfied with us, and we know that we will be satisfied with him."

John Paul has made no attempt to hide the points of divergence between Christians and Muslims, however, and has spoken bluntly about the most fundamental of those: what Christians believe about the person and work of Jesus of Nazareth. He said important differences should be accepted with humility and respect, in mutual tolerance. The practice of any faith must be conducted with respect for other religious traditions, because everyone hopes to be respected for what he or she is, and what he or she conscientiously believes.

The Pope's gestures are frequently as eloquent as his words, and a short visit to the Roman synagogue, Tempio Maggiore, in 1986 did more to do away with centuries of ill will between Catholics and Jews than have any documents or speeches. Significantly, in his talk at the synagogue, he spoke of Jews as the "elder brothers" of Christians. The Holy See's diplomatic recognition of the State of Israel in 1993, with the exchange of ambassadors, has also improved relations between the two immensely.

With *We Remember: A Reflection on the Shoah*, the Catholic Church's public examination of conscience about the Holocaust, another important step was taken. The ten-page document, written by the Vatican's Commission for Religious Relations with the Jews, was published in 1998 and approved by the Pope. "Did Christians give every possible assistance to those being persecuted, and in particular to the persecuted Jews?" the document asks. "Many did, but others did not."

Karol Wojtyla's friendship with Jews while he was growing up in Poland made him particularly sensitive to the Jewish people throughout his life. Jerzy Kluger, a Jewish friend of "Lolek" (a nickname for Karol), recalled him as a defender of local Jews, even as anti-Semitism began to surface in the days before World War II. Kluger told the story of a woman who, after finding the two young friends talking together in the Wadowice cathedral, questioned the presence of a Jew in church. Wojtyla laughed in response and asked, "Aren't we all God's children?"

*With Shimon Peres, former prime minister of Israel, Vatican City, 1992*

*With Rabbi Capo Elio Toaff, Tempio Maggiore Synagogue, Rome, 1986*

*With the Dalai Lama, Vatican City, 1990*

OTHER CHRISTIANS, OTHER RELIGIONS

elievers have a duty to treat all men and women
as brothers and sisters in the one human family;
prejudice and enmity have no place in true religion
and can never be justified on religious grounds.

*Address to the Ambassador of Great Britain, Vatican City, 1995*

OTHER CHRISTIANS, OTHER RELIGIONS

*Washington, D.C., 1979*

OTHER CHRISTIANS, OTHER RELIGIONS

Muslims, like Jews and Christians, see the figure of Abraham as a model of unconditional submission to the decrees of God. Following Abraham's example, the faithful strive to give God his rightful place in their lives as the origin, teacher, guide and ultimate destiny of all beings. This human docility and openness to God's will is translated into an attitude of prayer.

*May 5th General Audience, Vatican City, 1999*

The need of Christians for reconciliation with one another, for mutual forgiveness, is indeed great. Our search together in dialogue for ways to overcome the theological difficulties which stand in the way of Christian unity is a duty founded in the prayer of Christ himself for his disciples.

*Address to the Catholic-Pentecostal Commission, Vatican City, 1997*

The world is scandalized by divisions among Christians. As the year 2000 approaches, let us continue to listen to the word of God calling us to ever greater communion and cooperation. Our search for reconciliation therefore must go forward.

*Address to the Catholic-Pentecostal Commission, Vatican City, 1997*

*The Pope with the representatives of all the world religions, united for World Peace Day, Assisi, Italy, 1986*

T he commitment to ecumenism must be based upon the conversion of hearts and upon prayer, which will also lead to the necessary purification of past memories.

*Address to the Joint Committees of the Council of European Episcopal Conferences and the Conference of European Churches, Vatican City, 1998*

Called to overcome their fears, the Christian communities of various denominations are now invited to commit themselves courageously to the path that leads to full unity, to make a gift of their spiritual wealth and to share it in a trusting exchange. Christians will thus open the treasures of their spiritual life to the people of our time, who will be able to have a deeper encounter with the Lord.

*Address to the Joint Committees of the Council of European Episcopal Conferences and the Conference of European Churches, Vatican City, 1998*

The witness of unity is an essential element of an authentic and profound evangelization. Through their unity in the same Church, Christ's disciples will enable their brethren to discover the mystery of the Holy Trinity, the perfect communion of love. And we must remain restless until that time when, in docility to the Holy Spirit, we fulfill Christ's prayer: "That all may be one!"

*Address to the Joint Committees of the Council of European Episcopal Conferences and the Conference of European Churches, Vatican City, 1998*

Religious tolerance is based on the conviction that God wishes to be adored by people who are free: a conviction which requires us to respect and honor the inner sanctuary of conscience in which each person meets God.

*Greeting in Baltimore Cathedral, Maryland, 1995*

At the heart of every culture lies the attitude man takes to the greatest mystery: the mystery of God. Different cultures are basically different ways of facing the question of the meaning of personal existence.

*Centesimus Annus (The Hundredth Year), Vatican City, 1991*

*With the Patriarch of Constantinople, Rome, 1987*

OVERLEAF: *With Native American communities, Sault Sainte-Marie, Ontario, Canada, 1984*

OTHER CHRISTIANS, OTHER RELIGIONS

For John Paul II, the lay faithful fulfill their Christian vocation not just by going to church on Sunday but also within the worlds of work, recreation, sport, and social and family life. The Pope calls on Christians to be witnesses to their faith, especially in the workplace. Christ, the God-Man, worked as a carpenter along with St. Joseph, and those who follow him have the responsibility to be the leaven in every environment and every circumstance. The evangelization of the world—the spreading of the Gospel near and far—depends not only on missionaries, but also on the faithful and honest work carried out by ordinary Christians. They should respectfully but courageously tell others about Christ, John Paul writes, since "only in him is the answer to the most profound questions of every man and every woman."

For a long time in the Catholic Church, laypeople were defined by what they were *not*: They were all those baptized men and women who were not priests or members of religious orders. The word *layperson* somehow suggested second-class citizenship, as if bishops and priests, nuns, and monks ranked higher in God's eyes than did laypeople who had neither been ordained nor professed vows. That changed with the Second Vatican Council, which taught that there was an equality among the faithful in the Church. As one of the few prelates who attended all the Council sessions from 1962 through 1965, Karol Wojtyla was more aware than most of the changes taking place in Roman Catholicism. In addition, the Council, reviving an ancient tradition, labeled the Church the "People of God," and laymen and laywomen came to share more clearly in the mission of Christ. The universal call to holiness emerged as one of the key messages of Vatican II. The Council wrote that the vocation of ordinary men and women living and working in the world was to "seek the kingdom of God by engaging in temporal affairs and ordering them according to the plan of God."

While all the faithful are equal before God, different states in life lead people to seek holiness in different ways. Traditionally, many religious orders, such as those of cloistered nuns and monks, have separated themselves from ordinary life and preached a *contemptus mundi,* or contempt of the world, in an effort to seek the silence necessary for contemplation and union with God. For centuries, holiness had been regarded as the specific domain of priests and nuns. That has changed.

The Pope speaks of "vocation" not only in terms of a man becoming a priest or a woman professing vows in a religious community. Laypeople too receive a call to work for the greater glory of God, and the disciples of Christ no longer form a separate caste in the Catholic Church. They have come to include men and women in all walks of life, healthy and sick, young and old. Sanctity—striving for holiness—is for everyone.

ou therefore must be perfect as your heavenly Father is perfect" (Matthew 5:48). When he spoke those words in the fields, those who were listening to him were probably farm workers, housewives, craftsmen, beggars, shopkeepers, lawyers, children, priests, the sick. The Lord would have seen in them people of all ages, nationalities and professions.

*Address to Brazilian Bishops, Vatican City, 1995*

The "world" thus becomes the place and the means for the lay faithful to fulfill their Christian vocation, because the world itself is destined to glorify God the Father in Christ.

*Christifideles Laici (On the Vocation and Mission of the Laity), Vatican City, 1988*

*Gdansk , Poland, 1987*

$\mathbb{E}$veryone in the Church, precisely because they are members, receive and thereby share in the common vocation to holiness. In the fullness of this title and on equal par with all other members of the Church, the lay faithful are called to holiness.

*Christifideles Laici (On the Vocation and Mission of the Laity), Vatican City, 1988*

$\mathbb{T}$he new evangelization that can make the 21st century a spring-time of the Gospel is a task for the entire people of God, but will depend in a decisive way on the lay faithful being fully aware of their baptismal vocation and their responsibility for bringing the good news of Jesus Christ to their culture and society.

*Address to U.S. Bishops, Vatican City, 1998*

*Seoul, South Korea, 1984*

It is an inadequate understanding of the role of the laity which leads laymen and laywomen to become so strongly involved in Church services and tasks that they fail to become actively involved in their responsibilities in the professional, social, cultural and political fields.

*Address to U.S. Bishops, Vatican City, 1998*

LAYPEOPLE

The eyes of faith behold a wonderful scene: that of a countless number of laypeople, both women and men, busy at work in their daily life and activity, oftentimes far from view and quite unacclaimed by the world, unknown to the world's great personages but nonetheless looked upon in love by the Father, untiring laborers who work in the Lord's vineyard. Confident and steadfast through the power of God's grace, these are the humble yet great builders of the kingdom of God in history.

*Christifideles Laici (On the Vocation and Mission of the Laity), Vatican City, 1988*

Religious people who live in the world, but with a special consecration to God, will no longer be able to think that the laity can aspire to holiness despite the difficult conditions in which they live in the world, but on the contrary, they should consider that it is precisely through these difficulties that they are sanctified.

*Address to Brazilian Bishops, Vatican City, 1995*

There cannot be two parallel lives in their existence: on the one hand, the so-called "spiritual" life, with its values and demands; and on the other, the so-called "secular" life, that is, life in a family, at work, in social relationships, in the responsibilities of public life and in culture. . . . In fact, every area of the lay faithful's lives, as different as they are, enters into the plan of God. . . . Every activity, every situation, every precise responsibility . . . are the occasions ordained by Providence for a "continuous exercise of faith, hope and charity."

*Christifideles Laici (On the Vocation and Mission of the Laity), Vatican City, 1988*

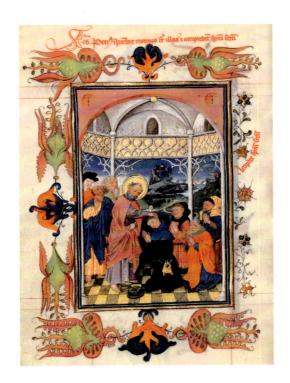

# III
# The Dignity of the Human Person

The Catholic Church teaches that every human being is composed of body and soul. It is the union of the body and the immortal soul, with its intellect and free will, that defines each person, who is unique and an expression of God's love. Although everyone must die, the soul is destined to live forever, and our bodies will rise again as well. Because human beings were made in the image and likeness of God and are destined for eternity, every human life is of infinite value.

*Japan, 1981*

ABOVE: *"Saint Peter Bestowing the Holy Ghost," from* The Book of Hours of Catherine of Cleves

he Pope believes that the world is engaged in a struggle between good and evil and that life issues form one of the battlefields. He sees a number of threats to human life in modern society, most notably abortion, contraception, and euthanasia, and feels compelled to stand in the first line of battle protecting the "culture of life" against the "culture of death." He has called on Catholics to make an unconditional defense of life, from conception to natural death, and wants to ensure against any dulling of consciences regarding what he calls "the seriousness of the crime of abortion."

Popes are expected to be countercultural, and John Paul II is no exception. What many developed countries have labeled rather coldly "the termination of a pregnancy," he has called a crime that cannot be morally justified by any circumstance or any law. At the same time, however, he has asked Catholics to help women in crisis pregnancies, and to counsel those who have had an abortion and may have to cope with its psychological and spiritual effects. This, too, is part of the culture of life. In the spirit of the Great Jubilee of the Year 2000, he said, Catholics should be more willing than ever to open their hearts and their homes

to unwanted and abandoned children, to young people in difficulty, to the handicapped, and to those who have no one to care for them.

Abortion has been one of John Paul's main concerns, and it was the primary reason the delegation from the Holy See was so active at the UN Conference on Population and Development in Cairo in 1994, repeatedly sparring with the United States. Rome recognizes that population growth has been dangerously high in some parts of the world, but insists that contraception and abortion are not the answer, and has been particularly critical of government sterilization programs. The Church teaches that only parents, and not any government authority, can determine how big a family should be. Nowhere does Catholic doctrine say that couples are obliged to have as many children as they possibly can. While the Church has condemned contraception, it does allow couples to space births by limiting sex to a woman's infertile periods.

In taking a stand that has alienated even many Catholics, the Pope has proclaimed Pope Paul VI's encyclical *Humanae Vitae* prophetic. The encyclical, written in 1968 with the help of Archbishop Wojtyla, declared the immorality of contraception among married couples. The Pope believes his predecessor correctly foresaw some of the consequences of separating married love from any possibility of producing life: a weakening of moral discipline, a trivialization of sexuality, the demeaning of women, marital infidelity, and broken homes.

The Pope believes that contemporary culture has a tendency to reduce life to a commodity. Marriage, in that context, can become simply a contract for sex, and one's husband or wife a mere object of pleasure. Catholic teaching on sex and reproduction has often been caricatured and badly misunderstood, and the Pope has requested that bishops and priests present it in a comprehensible and compelling way. Marriage-preparation programs, he says, should include an honest and complete presentation of the Church's teaching on what he calls "responsible procreation"— that is, the responsibility of parents to be generously open to life but not reckless in bringing into the world children they have neither the means nor the ability to raise.

John Paul's crusade for life goes far beyond abortion, contraception, and sterilization. He has reiterated Church teaching that euthanasia and assisted suicide are both grave violations of God's law. The Pontiff sees them as a direct threat to those least capable of defending themselves. On another front, traditional Church teaching has allowed for the death penalty in some cases as a way of protecting society from criminals, but John Paul has overseen an evolution in that teaching. The Universal Catechism states that if bloodless means are sufficient for a society to protect itself against an aggressor, the government should limit itself to such means. During his 1999 trip to St. Louis, the Pope even managed to save a convicted murderer from execution when he made an appeal to the Missouri governor, who granted the man clemency.

While opposition to the death penalty tends to be a position professed by political liberals and opposition to abortion decidedly not, John Paul sees a strong link among all life issues. If life is not respected at the beginning when it is most defenseless, who will protect the elderly, the infirm, the handicapped? He warns that "a society with a diminished sense of the value of human life at its earliest stages has already opened the door to a culture of death." Although abortion, euthanasia, and assisted suicide seem to be spreading rather than diminishing, the Pontiff hopes for change. Just as laws allowing slavery were overturned, John Paul says nations need the wisdom and courage to overcome the moral ills inherent in their march through history.

Life is one of the most beautiful titles which the Bible attributes to God. He is the living God.

*Message to the Pontifical Academy of Sciences, Vatican City, 1996*

While it is true that the taking of life not yet born or in its final stages is sometimes marked by a mistaken sense of altruism and human compassion, it cannot be denied that such a culture of death, taken as a whole, betrays a completely individualistic concept of freedom, which ends up by becoming the freedom of "the strong" against the weak who have no choice but to submit.

*Evangelium Vitae (The Gospel of Life), Vatican City, 1995*

The Church must proclaim the Gospel of life and speak out with prophetic force against the culture of death. May the Continent of Hope also be the Continent of Life! This is our cry: life with dignity for all! For all who have been conceived in their mother's womb, for street children, for indigenous peoples and African-Americans, for immigrants and refugees, for the young deprived of opportunity, for the old, for those who suffer any kind of poverty or marginalization.

*Homily, Mexico City, 1999*

$T$he Church counters the culture of death with the culture of love.

*Address to Brazilian Bishops, Vatican City, 1995*

*With Mother Teresa at her Nirmal Hriday Ashram, the House of the Pure Heart, Calcutta, 1986*

*St. Peter's Square, Vatican City, 1996*

The human person is a unique composite—a unity of spirit and matter, soul and body, fashioned in the image of God and destined to live forever. Every human life is sacred, because every human person is sacred. It is in the light of this fundamental truth that the Church constantly proclaims and defends the dignity of human life from the moment of conception to the moment of natural death.

*Message to Health Workers, Phoenix, Arizona, 1987*

It is possible to speak in a certain sense of a war of the powerful against the weak: a life which would require greater acceptance, love and care is considered useless, or held to be an intolerable burden, and is therefore rejected in one way or another. A person who, because of illness, handicap or, more simply, just by existing, compromises the well-being or lifestyle of those who are more favored tends to be looked upon as an enemy to be resisted or eliminated. In this way a kind of "conspiracy against life" is unleashed. This conspiracy involves not only individuals in their personal, family or group relationships, but goes far beyond, to the point of damaging and distorting, at the international level, relations between peoples and states.

*Evangelium Vitae (The Gospel of Life), Vatican City, 1995*

Life is always a good. This is an instinctive perception and a fact of experience, and man is called to grasp the profound reason why this is so. Why is life a good? This question is found everywhere in the Bible, and from the very first pages it receives a powerful and amazing answer. The life which God gives man is quite different from the life of all other living creatures, inasmuch as man, although formed from the dust of the earth, is a manifestation of God in the world, a sign of his presence, a trace of his glory.

*Evangelium Vitae (The Gospel of Life), Vatican City, 1995*

As part of the spiritual worship acceptable to God, the Gospel of life is to be celebrated above all in daily living, which should be filled with self-giving love for others. In this way, our lives will become a genuine and responsible acceptance of the gift of life and a heartfelt song of praise and gratitude to God who has given us this gift.

*Evangelium Vitae (The Gospel of Life), Vatican City, 1995*

*Turin, Italy, 1980*

# HUMAN RIGHTS

hile they are called "human" rights, the Catholic Church sees in them an intimate link with the divine. Human beings have inviolable, inalienable, and universal rights precisely because they are made in the image and likeness of God. It is their immortal souls that give people their dignity and make them different from all other earthly creatures. Human rights therefore stem naturally from the inherent worth of the human person, and are not merely a privilege conferred by a government or any other authority.

Pope John Paul II is frequently credited with having played a pivotal role in the downfall of Communism in Europe in the late 1980s. He would insist, however, that his words and actions—in support of the Polish labor union Solidarity, for example—were not against any one system, but in favor of the basic rights of every man and woman. For John Paul, these rights include a right to participate in social life, a right to truth, a right to free association and assembly, and various economic and professional rights. Despite the United Nations' Universal Declaration of Human Rights in 1948, societies have made little progress, because there are still countless people who suffer "violence, torture, terrorism, and discrimination in many forms," wrote John Paul in 1979 in his first encyclical, *The Redeemer of Man.*

For the Pope, a just and peaceful society depends on every member of that community or nation respecting the dignity of every other member and working for the common good: "When human rights are ignored or scorned, and when the pursuit of individual interests unjustly prevails over the common good, then the seeds of instability, rebellion and violence are inevitably sown."

Although all human rights are connected, the Pontiff considers the right to religious freedom the most basic, since it is founded on the relation between the creature and the Creator. John Paul calls religious freedom the heart of human rights, because religion expresses the deepest aspirations of people and helps shape their vision of the world. The Universal Declaration of Human Rights recognizes that the right to religious freedom includes the right to manifest personal beliefs, whether individually or with others, both in public and in private. Nevertheless, the authorities in several countries today deny freedom of worship. Christians have suffered terrible discrimination in several Islamic countries, most notably Saudi Arabia and the Sudan, and in Communist strongholds such as China and Cuba.

The Pontiff views as particularly grave state-sponsored discrimination that denies certain ethnic groups and national minorities their fundamental right to exist: "This is done by suppressing them or brutally forcing them to move, or by attempting to weaken their ethnic identity to such an extent that they are no longer distinguishable. Can we remain silent in the face of such grave crimes against humanity?" He applauded the efforts of the United Nations to establish an International Criminal Court to punish those responsible for crimes of genocide.

The Pope frequently promotes a "right to peace," since it ensures respect for all other rights and encourages the building of a society in which structures of power give way to structures of cooperation with a view to the common good. While differences in religious beliefs have at times triggered wars, John Paul condemns those conflicts, arguing that "recourse to violence in the name of religious belief is a perversion of the very teaching of the major religions."

War not only destroys, but also fails to resolve political and social problems without creating further divisions. "I think with sorrow of those living and growing up against a background of war, of those who have known nothing but conflict and violence," the Pope remarks. "Those who survive will carry the scars of this terrible experience for the rest of their lives." Children especially need peace, he points out, and they have the profoundest right to it. ▨

The dignity of the person is the indestructible property of every human being. The force of this affirmation is based on the uniqueness and irrepeatability of every person.

*Christifideles Laici (On the Vocation and Mission of the Laity), Vatican City, 1988*

It is a disquieting reflection on the state of human rights today that in some parts of the world people are still persecuted and imprisoned for reasons of conscience and for their religious beliefs. As innocent victims, they are sad proof that force and not democratic principles has prevailed, that the intention is not to serve the truth and the common good but to defend particular interests at any cost.

*Meeting with Muslims, Abuja, Nigeria, 1998*

There is a need for politicians, both men and women, who profoundly love their own people and wish to serve rather than be served. There can be no place for intimidation and domination of the poor and the weak, for arbitrary exclusion of individuals and groups from political life, for the misuse of authority or the abuse of power.

*Homily, Onitsha, Nigeria, 1998*

*Door through which slaves boarded ships, House of the Slaves, Gorée, Senegal, 1992*

 e must all work for a world in which no child will be deprived of peace and security, of a stable family life, of the right to grow up without fear and anxiety.

*Address at Departure Ceremonies,*
*Abuja, Nigeria, 1998*

*Kinshasa, Congo, 1980*

Many times, through the influence of the Spirit, prayer rises from the human heart in spite of prohibitions and persecutions and even official proclamations. . . . Prayer always remains the voice of all those who apparently have no voice.

*Dominum et Vivificantem (The Holy Spirit in the Life of the Church and the World), Vatican City, 1986*

Respect for the dignity of the person, which implies the defense and promotion of human rights, demands the recognition of the religious dimension of the individual. This is not simply a requirement "concerning matters of faith," but a reality that finds itself . . . bound up with the very reality of the individual. . . . Even if not all believe this truth, the many who are convinced of it have the right to be respected for their faith and for their life-choice, individual and communal, that flows from the faith. This is the right of freedom of conscience and religious freedom, the effective acknowledgement of which is among the highest goods and the most serious duties of every people that truly wishes to assure the good of the person and society.

*Christifideles Laici (On the Vocation and Mission of the Laity), Vatican City, 1988*

*Cebu Island, Philippines, 1981*

# SOLIDARITY

n 1988, Pope John Paul II created the virtue of solidarity. Although not new as a word or idea, the Pope made it a virtue along the lines of honesty, loyalty, and generosity, and described it as the "firm and persevering determination to commit oneself to the common good." It demands more than giving old clothes or extra food to the poor; solidarity requires a constant effort to help those who are less fortunate.

Many people have thought John Paul's interest in the theme of solidarity was born with the Polish labor union of the same name, Solidarity, which was so instrumental in the nonviolent overthrow of the Communists in his homeland, but that is not the case. The word *solidarity* has been used by Catholic thinkers for decades to distinguish Catholic social doctrine from both Communism and liberal capitalism. The Pope has tried taking it a step further, out of the textbooks and into the hearts and minds of all Christians.

Global solidarity means concern for the developing world, and John Paul has shown special attention to Africa. When the Pope touched down in Cameroon, South Africa, and Kenya in September 1995, it marked the 11th time he had traveled to the vast continent as Pontiff. And he has been back, with a second visit to Nigeria in 1998. While much of the world's attention has been focused on Europe during his pontificate, John Paul will not allow Africa to be forgotten.

John Paul has compared the African continent to the robbery victim who has been beaten and left by the side of the road in the Gospel parable. The Good Samaritan comes to take care of him. "Africa is a continent where countless human beings—men and women, children and young people—are lying, as it were, on the edge of the road, sick, injured, disabled, marginalized, and abandoned. They are in dire need of Good Samaritans who will come to their aid."

Africa is filled with lights and shadows for the Catholic Church. Alongside seminaries bursting at the seams and countless vocations among both men and women is a terrible shortage of educational facilities and financial means. While brutal civil wars continue to scar several nations on the continent, John Paul has praised the positive values that have allowed Christianity to flourish in parts of Africa, even though missionaries arrived in some countries only a hundred years ago. He points particularly to a profound religious sense among Africans and their strong belief in the fundamental role of the family. "The peoples of Africa respect the life that is conceived and born," he says. "They reject the idea that it can be destroyed."

The Pope's concern for the developing world goes far beyond Africa, however; he wants to instill a sense of solidarity for the entire Southern Hemisphere. He has said the Jubilee Year 2000 could be an appropriate time to substantially reduce or cancel altogether Third World debt, which has kept so many countries from making progress. In a 1988 encyclical, *Concern for the Social Order,* the Pontiff noted the crippling worldwide problems created by the unequal distribution of wealth. He believes that political leaders and citizens of rich countries, especially if they are Christians, have the moral obligation to use their wealth to alleviate the suffering of the world's poor. For John Paul, the fulfillment of this obligation is central to achieving the common good that is solidarity's highest goal.

OVERLEAF: *St. Peter's Square, Vatican City, 1983*

ower is responsibility: it is service, not privilege. Its exercise is morally justifiable when it is used for the good of all, when it is sensitive to the needs of the poor and defenseless.

*Evening Prayer, St. Louis, Missouri, 1999*

olidarity helps us to see the "other"—whether a person, people or nation—not just as some kind of instrument, with a work capacity and physical strength to be exploited at low cost and then discarded when no longer useful, but as our "neighbor," a "helper" to be made a sharer, on a par with ourselves, in the banquet of life to which all are equally invited by God.

*Sollicitudo Rei Socialis (On Social Concern), Vatican City, 1987*

o prevent the globalization of the economy from producing the harmful results of an uncontrolled expansion of private or group interests, it is necessary that the progressive globalization of the economy be increasingly met with a "global" culture of solidarity attentive to the needs of the weakest.

*Address to the Centesimus Annus—Pro-Pontifice Foundation, Vatican City, 1998*

*Mass at Mount Hagen, Papua New Guinea , 1984*

OVERLEAF: *Majdanek concentration camp, Poland, 1987*

I**t** was not understood that a society worthy of the person is not built by destroying the person, by repression and by discrimination. This lesson of the Second World War has not yet been learned completely and in all quarters. And yet it remains and must stand as a warning for the next millennium.

*Message on the Fiftieth Anniversary of the End of World War II, Vatican City, 1995*

Today perhaps more than in the past, people are realizing that they are linked together by a common destiny, which is to be constructed together, if catastrophe for all is to be avoided. From the depth of anguish, fear and escapist phenomena like drugs, typical of the contemporary world, the idea is slowly emerging that the good to which we are all called and the happiness to which we aspire cannot be obtained without an effort and commitment on the part of all, nobody excluded, and the consequent renouncing of personal selfishness.

*Sollicitudo Rei Socialis (On Social Concern), Vatican City, 1987*

At this point we have to ask ourselves if the sad reality of today might not be, at least in part, the result of a too narrow idea of development, that is, a mainly economic one.

*Sollicitudo Rei Socialis (On Social Concern), Vatican City, 1987*

We need first of all to foster, in ourselves and in others, a contemplative outlook. Such an outlook arises from faith in the God of life, who has created every individual as a "wonder." This outlook does not give in to discouragement when confronted by those who are sick, suffering, outcast or at death's door. Instead, in all these situations it feels challenged to find meaning, and precisely in these circumstances it is open to perceiving in the face of every person a call to encounter, dialogue and solidarity.

*Evangelium Vitae (The Gospel of Life), Vatican City, 1995*

The exercise of solidarity within each society is valid when its members recognize one another as persons. Those who are more influential, because they have a greater share of goods and common services, should feel responsible for the weaker and be ready to share with them all they possess. Those who are weaker, for their part, in the same spirit of solidarity, should not adopt a purely passive attitude or one that is destructive of the social fabric, but, while claiming their legitimate rights, should do what they can for the good of all.

*Sollicitudo Rei Socialis (On Social Concern), Vatican City, 1987*

It is timely to mention—and it is no exaggeration—that a leadership role among nations can only be justified by the possibility and willingness to contribute widely and generously to the common good.

*Sollicitudo Rei Socialis (On Social Concern), Vatican City, 1987*

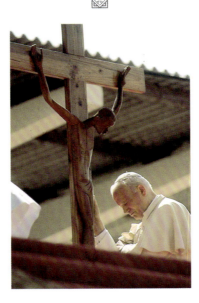

*Angola, 1992*

reedom, for John Paul II, has an essential link to the truth, which is God. It does not mean doing what you want, but doing what is right. The great violence of the 20th century—two world wars and scores of other bloody conflicts—has been caused in large part, he argues, because people have lost sight of the ultimate truth of God. When that happens, anything goes.

The Pope talked at length about freedom and its relation to the truth in a 1998 address to the United States Ambassador to the Holy See. He did not cite the great Catholic authors and saints, such as Augustine and Aquinas, but rather the Founding Fathers of the United States.

He referred to their claim to freedom on the basis of certain self-evident truths about the human person, and also mentioned the "ordered liberty" of George Washington. "Reading the founding documents of the United States, one has to be impressed by the concept of freedom they enshrine," he said, "a freedom designed to enable people to fulfill their duties and responsibilities toward the family and toward the common good of the community. The authors clearly understood that there could be no true freedom without moral responsibility and accountability."

He told the ambassador that the best expression of a society's commitment to "liberty and justice for all" is the protection of the most vulnerable. "The United States of America was founded on the conviction that an inalienable right to life was a self-evident moral truth, fidelity to which was a primary criterion of social justice," he said. "Whenever a certain category of people—the unborn or the sick and old—are excluded from that protection, a deadly anarchy subverts the original understanding of justice."

When countries enjoy periods of wealth and freedom, they need to act in a responsible manner toward other nations. "Peace and prosperity, in fact, are goods that belong to the whole human race," he wrote in the encyclical *Centesimus Annus* (The Hundredth Year), written shortly after the fall of the Berlin Wall. "It is not possible to enjoy them in a proper and lasting way if they are achieved and maintained at the cost of other peoples and nations, by violating their rights or excluding them from the sources of well-being."

In *Centesimus Annus,* John Paul recognized the importance of economic freedom and private initiative. He stressed that economic freedom was important, but that it could not be used at the expense of others. Stronger nations need to find ways to offer weaker ones opportunities for taking their rightful place in international life: "Economic freedom is only one element of human freedom. When man is seen more as a producer or consumer of goods than as a subject who produces and consumes in order to live, then economic freedom loses its necessary relationship to the human person and ends up by alienating and oppressing him."

John Paul coined the term "victims of consumerism" and affirms that what you are is infinitely more important than what you own. He wrote that "it is not wrong to want to live better. What is wrong is a style of life that is presumed to be better when it is directed toward 'having' rather than 'being.'" Someone might be very rich, and have hundreds of people working for him, but still be essentially a slave. "A person who is concerned solely or primarily with possessing and enjoying, who is no longer able to control his instincts and passions . . . cannot be free."

John Paul talks about an "obedience to the truth about God and man" as the first condition of freedom. Only then can someone order his or her needs and desires and choose the means of satisfying them according to a correct scale of values. And only then can he or she be truly happy, since freedom is related to the truth, and the truth is intimately linked to happiness.

**M**an cannot be forced to accept the truth. He can be drawn toward the truth only by his own nature, that is, by his own freedom, which commits him to search sincerely for truth and, when he finds it, to adhere to it both in his convictions and his behavior.

*Crossing the Threshold of Hope, 1994*

**O**ur society must be vigilant if it is to avoid the recurrence of totalitarian ideologies, because they offend the dignity of every individual and foster rejection of the portion of humanity that does not belong to a specific culture or religion.

*Address to Members of the Pax Christi Movement, Vatican City, 1995*

**F**reedom is not the ability to do anything we want, whenever we want. Rather, freedom is the ability to live responsibly the truth of our relationship with God and with one another.

*Address to Youth, St. Louis, Missouri, 1999*

*Managua, Nicaragua, 1983*

OVERLEAF: *Angola, 1992*

MEMBER OF

JOÃO PAULO II

**R**evelation teaches that the power to decide what is good and what is evil does not belong to man, but to God alone. Man is certainly free, inasmuch as he can understand and accept God's commands. And he possesses an extremely far-reaching freedom, since he can eat "of every tree of the garden." But his freedom is not unlimited: it must halt before the "tree of the knowledge of good and evil," for it is called to accept the moral law given by God. In fact, human freedom finds its authentic and complete fulfillment precisely in the acceptance of that law. God, who alone is good, knows perfectly what is good for man, and by virtue of his very love proposes this good to man in the commandments.

*Veritatis Splendor (The Splendor of the Truth), Vatican City, 1993*

**N**owadays it is sometimes held, though wrongly, that freedom is an end in itself, that each human being is free when he makes use of freedom as he wishes, and that this must be our aim in the lives of individuals and societies. In reality, freedom is a great gift only when we know how to use it consciously for everything that is our true good. Christ teaches us that the best use of freedom is charity, which takes concrete form in self-giving and in service.

*Redemptor Hominis (The Redeemer of Man), Vatican City, 1979*

*Washington, D.C., 1979*

othing, insists John Paul II, is resolved by war. Rather, it aggravates old tensions and creates new ones, placing everything in jeopardy. After so many unnecessary massacres, he pleads with peoples and nations to recognize once and for all "that war never helps the human community, that violence destroys and never builds up, that the wounds it causes remain long unhealed." The Pope seems to suggest that the circumstances that once allowed for traditional Catholic teaching on a "just war" are no longer valid in the age of modern warfare.

Peace, for John Paul, is built on the premise of respect for the freedom and rights of other individuals and groups. "Wars continue to break out and destruction has fallen upon peoples and whole cultures because the sovereignty of a people or nation was not respected," he wrote at the beginning of his pontificate. "Every continent has seen and suffered from wars and struggles caused by one nation's attempt to limit another's auton-

omy." While patriotism is a virtue, Christian teaching condemns all forms of nationalism and doctrines of cultural supremacy, which have often triggered wars and continue to do so today.

The globalization of the economy and the rapid progress of information technologies have led the Pope to remark that these changes have triggered both great hopes and disturbing questions about the future of humanity. Some of his own questions are these: Will *everyone* be able to take advantage of a global market? Will *everyone* at last have a chance to enjoy peace? Will relations between nations become more equitable, or will economic competition and rivalries between peoples and nations lead humanity toward a situation of even greater instability?

Poverty and peace are related, and this connection is what led John Paul to title one of his messages for the World Day of Prayer for Peace, *If You Want Peace, Reach Out to the Poor.* Poverty represents a clear threat to peace, because it often prevents countries and entire regions from maintaining stability. In certain countries in Africa, Asia, and Latin

America, vast sectors of the population live on the margins of society and are therefore excluded from the benefits that should be shared by all. A nation, whatever its political or economic system, remains fragile and unstable if it does not give constant attention to its weakest members. A government must ensure that at least the primary needs of all its people—housing, work, education—are satisfied.

Just as poor people have a claim on the attention of the affluent, poor countries have a "right to development," and John Paul calls on wealthier nations to show them solidarity. "The Church's admonition is clear, and it is a faithful echo of the voice of Christ," he writes. "Earthly goods are meant for the whole human family and cannot be reserved for the exclusive benefit of a few."

"Violence never builds up," says the Pontiff, with one exception. It never builds anything but poverty. War increases the sufferings of the poor, and creates new poor by destroying homes and property and means of subsistence. "Women, children, the elderly, the sick and the wounded are forced to flee and become refugees who have no possessions beyond what they can carry with them," he has stated. "Helpless and defenseless, they seek refuge in other countries or regions that are often as poor and turbulent as their own."

The Pope encourages all those who believe in God to pray for peace, since prayer is the bond that most effectively unites them. Through prayer, believers meet one another before God, the Lord and Father of all, before whom all inequalities, misunderstandings, bitterness and hostility can be overcome. "Peace be with you," were the first words of the risen Christ to the Apostles, and the Pope laments that two thousand years later there are still wars of savage intensity being fought on almost every continent. While there is a need for negotiations and diplomacy, peace really begins in one's own heart. Only when someone is at peace, or friendship, with God, can he or she be at peace with others.

OVERLEAF: *Onitsha, Nigeria, 1982*

Peace flows from justice, and justice is dependent on truth, the truth concerning God and concerning the meaning and purpose of human life, for we have been created in the image and likeness of God himself.

*Address to the Cadets of the New York Maritime College, Vatican City, 1995*

Neither the reduction in the number of weapons, disarmament, nor the absence of war leads immediately to peace. It is essential to create a culture of life and a culture of peace. This is an apprenticeship that must start very early in the family and in the different areas of education. In fact, we become accustomed to peace-building behavior when we learn to respect those who are close to us, when we train ourselves to resolve conflicts peacefully between people who live together and when we foster gestures of forgiveness which dispel aggressive attitudes. Therefore parents have an invaluable role to play in creating a harmonious family atmosphere, favorable to helping young people to mature, and to put in their hearts the desire to seek peace despite everything.

*Address to Members of the Pax Christi Movement, Vatican City, 1995*

*Pope John Paul II signs a peace agreement between Argentina and Chile in the Sala Concistoro, Vatican City, 1984*

One cannot remain a prisoner of the past, for individuals and peoples need a sort of "healing of memories," so that past evils will not come back again. This does not mean forgetting past events; it means reexamining them with a new attitude and learning precisely from the experience of suffering that only love can build up, whereas hatred produces devastation and ruin.

*Message for World Day of Peace, Vatican City, 1997*

Reconciliation is not weakness or cowardice. On the contrary, it demands courage and sometimes even heroism; it is victory over self rather than over others. It should never be seen as dishonor. For in reality it is the patient, wise art of peace.

*Homily, Onitsha, Nigeria, 1998*

Whenever violence is done in the name of religion, we must make it clear to everyone that in such instances we are not dealing with true religion.

*Meeting with Muslims, Abuja, Nigeria, 1998*

KOSOVO 1999

3600   Città del Vaticano

Il Papa sta con il popolo
che soffre, e a tutti grida:
è sempre l'ora della pace!

*Joannes Paulus PP II*

COURVOISIER

*A 1999 Vatican City postage stamp commemorating the refugees of Kosovo reads: "The Pope is with the people who suffer and shouts to everyone: It is always time for peace!"*

€thnic and cultural differences should never be seen as justifying conflict. Rather, like the various voices in a choir, these differences can exist in harmony, provided there is a real desire to respect one another.

*Meeting with Muslims, Abuja, Nigeria, 1998*

# SUFFERING & EVIL

At the heart of Christianity is the theme of salvation—saving one's body and soul from eternal damnation. To save, writes the Pope, means to liberate from evil, especially from radical, ultimate evil. When Christ redeemed humanity through his cross and resurrection, death ceased to be an ultimate evil, and became subject to the power of life. And yet, real evil—genocide, wars, violence against children—continues to disfigure the face of humanity. If God is love, as the Gospel says, why does evil run rampant through the world? If he is the Lord of life, why does the world seem bent on death and destruction?

Again, the answer lies somewhere in the heart of every human being. Sin is the source of every evil, and no human being, with the exception of the Virgin Mary, has been preserved from sin. As a result of original sin, all men and women have what is called in Latin the *fomes peccati,* or inclination to do what they know to be wrong. They commit sins despite their conscience, because passions of all kinds—for power, for money, for pleasure—overpower reason. Without grace, and the struggle to overcome their fallen nature, men and women are capable of the worst evils imaginable. While there is a tendency to think of real evil only in terms of genocide, Catholic theology teaches that it can be much more subtle. For instance, what are known as the seven deadly sins—pride, avarice, envy, wrath, lust, gluttony, and sloth—do not even sound so terrible, but they are the fundamental disorientations we find in ourselves, and lead to a host of sinful actions.

God could have created man to do only good and no evil. But then man would not have been free. God, who is all-powerful, chose to make himself powerless in the face of human freedom, John Paul II reasons. However, the price of freedom is terribly high, since freedom brings with it pain, injustice, and all suffering great and small. But also with free will comes merit. It is merit that leads us either to gain a place among the blessed in heaven, or to be condemned to hell. Eternal damnation, says the Pope, does not mean that God rejects an individual, but that this individual has freely rejected God.

Had there been no sin, no original sin, there would have been no suffering in the world. Nor would there have been death. With original sin, the human race lost the beautiful harmony it had had with God. Man became subject to sickness and death, and his fallen nature made him prone to the greatest evil of all—sin, or enmity with God. But the Pope teaches that Christ has made suffering the firm basis of the most definitive good that man can achieve—eternal salvation. It was only through the cross that the gates of heaven were opened.

Most people protest the sufferings they have to endure. John Paul, who has faced tremendous trials in his own life, beginning with the loss of his mother, father, and only brother before he was 21 years old, encourages those who are suffering to look for the spiritual meaning of what at first appears inexplicable. One can understand more about pain when one meditates on the sufferings of Christ, perfect God and perfect man, and the most innocent victim. If united with the passion of Christ, suffering is no longer seen as useless. It is a sign of the salvation to come. The Pope remarks that if a person understands the supernatural significance of his or her suffering, it can even be a source of joy.

While the Pope acknowledges that the mystery of sin often wields tremendous power in the world, he describes himself as someone who has both joy and hope, and believes deeply in the value of existence and the hope of a future life. "Do not be conquered by evil but conquer evil with good," St. Paul wrote to the Romans. And the Pope insists that the possibility to do good is greater than all the evil in the world. Evil may be a harsh reality, but it is not definitive, and with grace and a responsible use of his freedom, man can overcome it. God's love can conquer any evil, and this lays the foundation for a Christian's hope and joy.

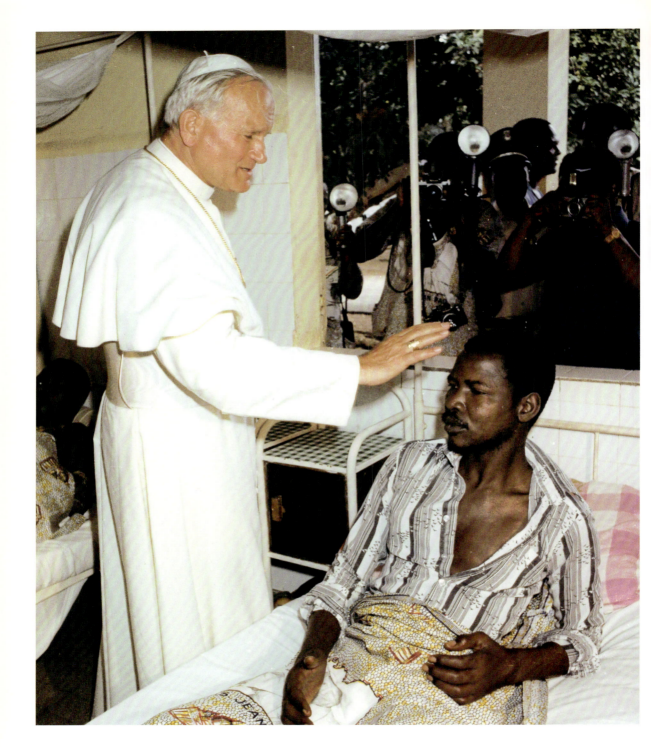

*J*esus did not hesitate to proclaim the blesssedness of those who suffer. . . . This blessedness can only be understood if one admits that human life is not limited to the time spent on earth, but is wholly directed to perfect joy and fullness of life in the hereafter. Earthly suffering, when accepted in love, is like a bitter kernel containing the seed of new life, the treasure of divine glory to be given man in eternity.

*April 27th General Audience, Vatican City, 1994*

*I*n their lives, in order to respect fundamental values, Christians also experience that suffering which can result from moral choices opposed to worldly behavior and which therefore can be heroic. But this is the price of the life of blessed happiness with the Lord.

*Message for World Youth Day, Paris, 1997*

*S*uffering, in fact, is always a great test not only of physical strength but also of spiritual strength. . . . Prayer for the suffering and with the suffering is therefore a special part of this great cry that the Church and the Pope raise together with Christ. It is a cry for the victory of good even through evil, through suffering, through every worrying and human injustice.

*Crossing the Threshold of Hope, 1994*

*Ivory Coast, 1980*

People react to suffering in different ways. But in general it can be said that almost always the individual enters suffering with a typically human protest and with the question "why." He asks the meaning of his suffering and seeks an answer to this question on the human level. Certainly he often puts this question to God, and to Christ. Furthermore, he cannot help noticing that the one to whom he puts the question is himself suffering and wishes to answer him from the cross, from the heart of his own suffering. Nevertheless, it often takes time, even a long time, for this answer to begin to be interiorly perceived. . . . Man hears Christ's saving answer as he himself gradually becomes a sharer in the sufferings of Christ.

*Salvifici Doloris (On the Christian Meaning of Human Suffering), Vatican City, 1984*

Apart from faith, pain has always been a great riddle of human existence. Ever since Jesus, however, redeemed the world by his passion and death, a new perspective has been opened: through suffering one can grow in self-giving and attain the highest degree of love (John 13:1), because of him who "loved us and gave himself for us" (Ephesians 5:2).

*April 27th General Audience, Vatican City, 1994*

In order to perceive the true answer to the "why" of suffering, we must look to the revelation of divine love, the ultimate source of the meaning of everything that exists. Love is also the richest source of the meaning of suffering, which always remains a mystery: we are conscious of the insufficiency and inadequacy of our explanations. Christ causes us to enter into the mystery and to discover the "why" of suffering, as far as we are capable of grasping the sublimity of divine love.

*Salvifici Doloris (On the Christian Meaning of Human Suffering), Vatican City, 1984*

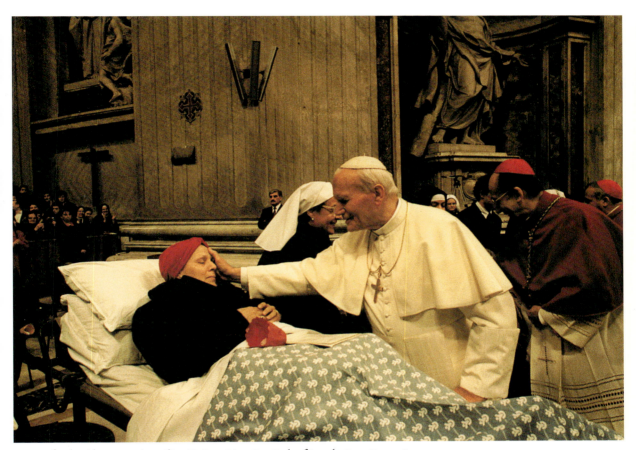

*A Mass for the sick, St. Peter's Basilica, Vatican City,  Our Lady of Lourdes Feast Day, 1985*

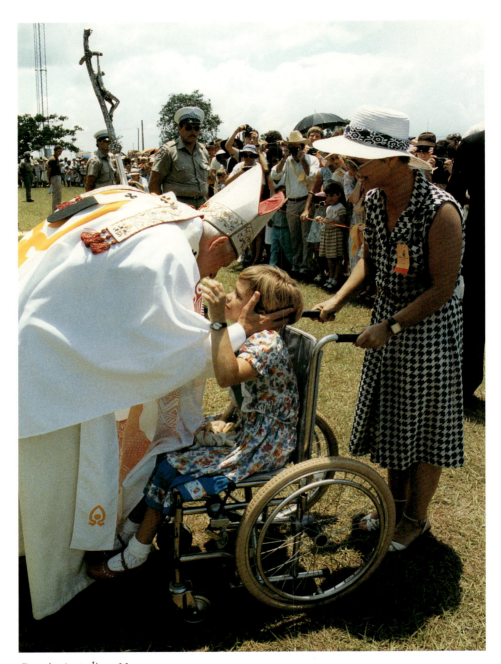

*Darwin, Australia, 1986*

**B**efore sin man possessed sanctifying grace with all the supernatural gifts that make man "righteous" before God. We may sum up all this by saying that at the beginning, man was in friendship with God.

*General Audience Concerning the Catechesis of Original Sin, Vatican City, 1996*

**I**n suffering there is concealed a particular power that draws a person interiorly close to Christ. . . . A result of such a conversion is not only that the individual discovers the salvific meaning of suffering but above all that he becomes a completely new person. He discovers a new dimension, as it were, of his entire life and vocation. This discovery is a particular confirmation of the spiritual greatness which in man surpasses the body in a way that is completely beyond compare. When this body is gravely ill, totally incapacitated, and the person is almost incapable of living and acting, all the more do interior maturity and spiritual greatness become evident, constituting a touching lesson to those who are healthy and normal.

*Salvifici Doloris (On the Christian Meaning of Human Suffering), Vatican City, 1984*

OVERLEAF: *The Hill of Crosses memorial was built and rebuilt many times for those who were imprisoned, sent to concentration camps, deported to Siberia, and condemned to death. Siauliai, Lithuania, 1993*

# IV
# A Lifetime of Devotion

Karol Wojtyla's early years were spent in a setting much like that of any child growing up in Poland at the time, with a loving and religious family life and the usual schoolboy friendships. But tragedy entered his life at the age of eight when his mother died after a short illness. The death of his older brother Edmund only four years later, and his father's death in the first year of World War II, left Karol Wojtyla with no immediate family before he turned 21. Despite the loss of his loved ones, he was an amiable boy and continued to enjoy the pleasures of childhood and youth. He had a number of good friends with whom he shared a love of sports, particularly soccer. In his teens, he developed a passion for both literature and theater and was considered an excellent actor. He was equally passionate about nature and cherished the time he could spend outdoors, canoeing, hiking, and skiing as much as possible.

John Paul II's spiritual roots lie in a distinctly Polish approach to Catholicism; his deep piety and unwavering devotion to Mary can be traced to his parents and his beloved homeland, where Mary is "Queen." This faith and devotion were forged by his early family life and would be tested and strengthened as he witnessed firsthand the horrors his country suffered, first under Nazi occupation and later under Communist control.

From an early age, John Paul had an avid interest in the world beyond his native nation. He became a student—of other peoples, other languages, other lands—of what one of his aides calls "human geography." As a young priest, he perfected his French, Latin, and Greek, and later he learned Italian, German, and English. He studied Spanish in order to read in the original the works of one of his favorite mystics, St. John of the Cross. From the time he became a bishop, he traveled extensively, a practice that would serve him well as pastor of the Universal Church.

1921
One-year-old Karol Jozef Wojtyla, known as "Lolus" as an infant and then as "Lolek."

**1904**

Karol Wojtyla Sr., a 25-year-old noncommissioned administrative officer in the Austrian army, married 21-year-old Emilia Kaczorowska, a Silesian of Lithuanian origin, on February 10, 1904, in Kraków. They settled in Wadowice in Galicia, the southern province of Poland, after their marriage. Both were deeply devout.

**1908**

The Pope's parents, with his elder brother Edmund, around 1908. Edmund would study medicine, and as a young doctor he became fatally infected with scarlet fever. He died at the age of 26 in 1932.

**1920**

Karol was born in Wadowice, Poland on May 18, 1920. This photo of him with his mother was taken a few months later. She died when he was only eight years old.

**1929**

OPPOSITE: Karol on the day of his First Communion at age nine in 1929.

1 9 3 0

Karol (back row left) with his classmates at grammar school. He is
remembered as a very good student with a particular fondness for
patriotic literature and theater.

1 9 3 1

At the age of 11, Karol (front row, second from left) became an
altar boy. Almost immediately, he was put in charge of the other
altar boys. He would often serve two or even three Masses a day.

1 9 3 2

Karol at age 12, the year he lost
his beloved brother Edmund—
another profound blow.

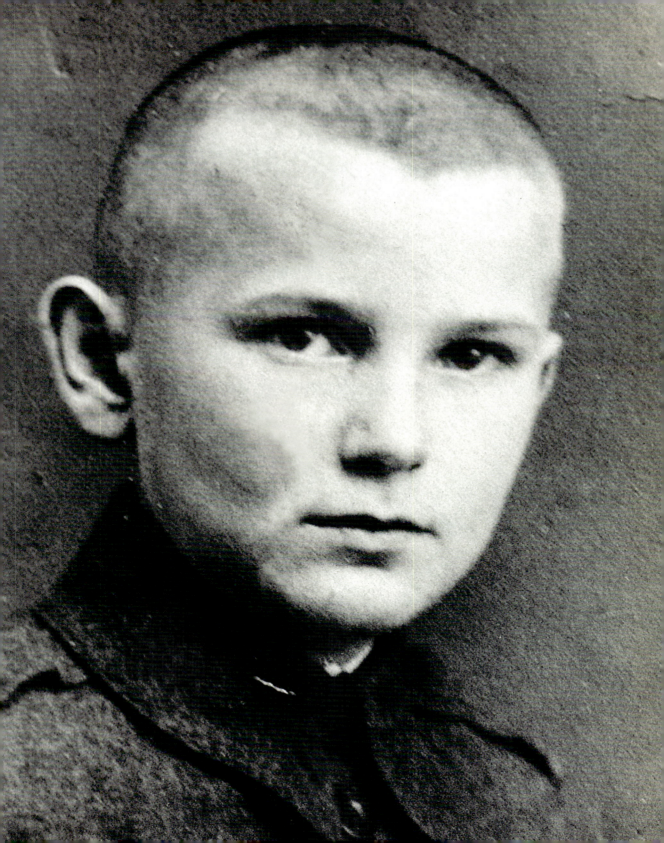

1939

In 1939, together with his friends, Wojtyla founded the student theater group "Studio 39." They wrote, staged, and performed their own plays, even when the Nazi invasion forced them underground. Both photos were taken during this time. The photo above was used in one of the group's posters.

**1939–1942**

John Paul II is the first Pope to have spent part of his life as an industrial worker. Here he is shown (second from right) building a school in Ukraine, as part of the Academic Legion military program in which he participated in 1939. Wojtyla had had only one year of normal study at Kraków's prestigious Jagiellonian University—Nicolaus Copernicus and Vladimir Lenin studied there—before war broke out and the Nazis closed down the universities and seminaries. In order to survive, while continuing to study in secret, he worked in a quarry breaking up stones for eight hours a day of hard physical labor, working outside even in freezing weather. Later, his job in a water purification plant required carrying buckets of lime on a wooden yoke.

**1939**

Wojtyla (first row, second from right) completed his required military service as a member of the Academic Legion. Along with his fellow student cadets, he was sent to a training camp in Ukraine in the summer of 1939. He was released and returned home shortly before the Nazis invaded Poland in September of that year. Barely one year later his father died. The grief-stricken Karol, now left without immediate family, prayed beside his father's body for twelve hours.

In 1942, at the age of 22, Wojtyla approached the archbishop of Kraków, Adam Sapieha, and stated flatly: "I want to be a priest." He became a student of theology in the underground seminary run by the archbishop and in 1944 was saved from the Nazis by hiding in the archbishop's palace. He was ordained in 1946 (right). Above, he sits with the children from his first parish in Niegoszowice.

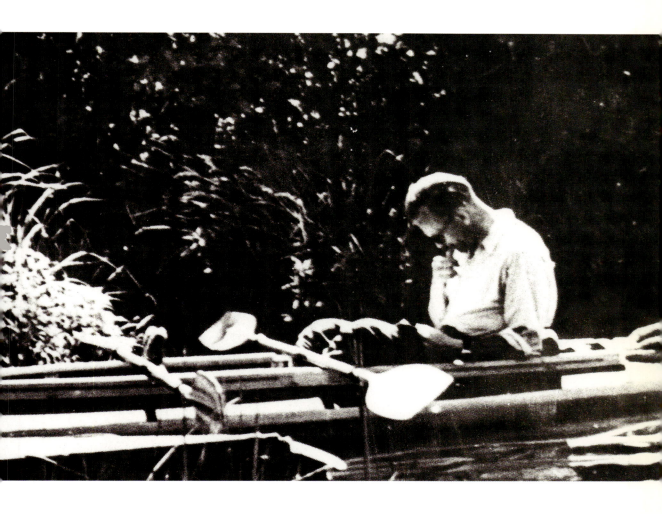

Throughout his life, Wojtyla had always been an avid sportsman. He loved soccer and would often go hiking, kayaking, or bicycling in the mountains in southern Poland. He was also a very good skier and a tough mountain climber. He continued these activities as a young priest, and later when he was made a cardinal. He always carried a portable altar when he was camping, and would make a cross by lashing together two paddles.

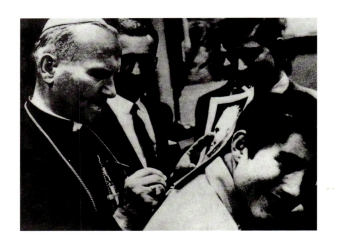

1958–1967

Wojtyla's rise through the Church hierarchy was swift and brilliant. He was named auxiliary bishop in 1958, then archbishop and metropolitan of Kraków in 1964, and then cardinal in 1967. Wojtyla was a frequent visitor to Rome both during and after the Second Vatican Council (1962–1965) for consultations with other bishops and cardinals. His work for the Vatican afforded him travel to many other places as well. He was wildly popular wherever he went.

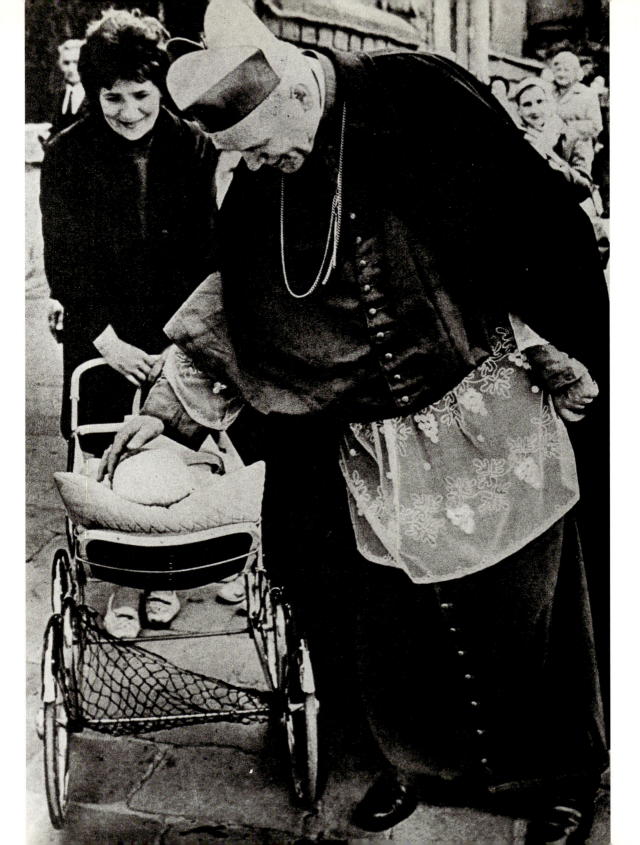

1967–1978

Karol Wojtyla during the
time he was archbishop of
Kraków. He was a fearless
defender of the Church
against the Communist party.

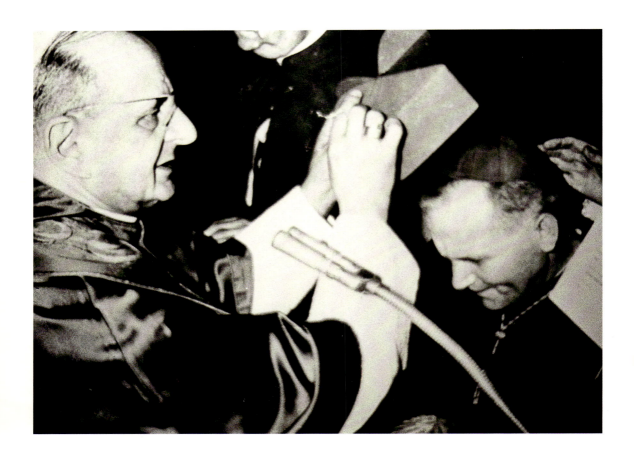

1978

In photo at right, Cardinal Wojtyla pays homage to Pope John Paul I
on the occasion of John Paul I's election and investiture. Less than
two months later, Wojtyla would be Pope himself. Both Wojtyla and
Albino Luciani, who was Pope John Paul I for 33 days, were appointed
cardinals by Pope Paul VI (above at left). Wojtyla chose the name
John Paul II in honor of his predecessor.

## 1 9 7 8

On October 16th, 1978, only two days after the cardinals convened in the Sistine Chapel, the white smoke rising from the chapel's chimney announced they had chosen a new Pope. One hour later, John Paul II appeared on the balcony of St. Peter's (above). The first non-Italian Pope in four and a half centuries spoke his first official words in fluent Italian: "*Sia lodato Gesù Cristo*" ("Praised be Jesus Christ").

John Paul is one of the most beloved religious leaders of the 20th century. His dramatic and vigorous tenure, now in its third decade, has resulted in profound changes in the Catholic Church and throughout the world. He is an ardent spokesman for human dignity and a beacon of hope for the 21st century.

*St. Peter's Basilica, Vatican City, 1985*

A LIFETIME OF DEVOTION

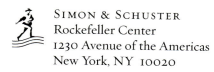

SIMON & SCHUSTER
Rockefeller Center
1230 Avenue of the Americas
New York, NY 10020

Printed in China by Palace Press International

10 9 8 7 6 5 4 3 2 1

Library of Congress Cataloging-in-Publication Data is available.

ISBN 0-684-87033-9

Unless otherwise noted, all selections from the Pope's writings and speeches have been taken from the official Vatican English-language translations of papal documents. The literary style and punctuation of the Vatican have been adhered to.

Text excerpts on pp. 105, 176, and 193 from *Crossing the Threshold of Hope* by His Holiness John Paul II. Translation copyright © 1994 by Alfred A. Knopf, Inc. Reprinted by permission of the publisher.

## PICTURE CREDITS

© Archivio Bigazzi: pp. 208 and 209; © Arnaud de Wildenberg/Gamma: back jacket; © Catholic Press Photo: pp. 5 (bottom), 16–17, 46, 68, 106–107, 112–113, 152, 200, 202 (3 photos), 203, 204 (2 photos), 206; © David Burnett/Contact Press Images: front jacket; © CORBIS/Bettmann-UPI: p. 121; © Fondazione Casa di Giovanni Paolo II, Wadowice: p. 214 (top); © Fotografia Felici S.n.c.: p. 116 (left); © François Lochon/Gamma: pp. 4 (bottom), 18–19, 33, 38–39, 50–51, 58–59, 61, 69, 70, 79, 86, 90–91, 93, 94–95, 132, 138–139, 160–161, 162–163, 168–169, 177, 184–185, 220; © Gamma: pp. 116 (center), 205, 210, 211, 212 (bottom), 214 (bottom), 218; © Giancarlo Giuliani/Edizioni San Paolo: pp. 4 (top), 5 (top), 26, 47, 66, 102–103, 134, 146, 158, 173, 178–179; © Gianni Giansanti/Sygma: pp. 6–7, 10–11, 20–21, 30–31, 54, 101, 109, 110, 118, 166–167, 198–199, 223; © Interpress Polska/Gamma: pp. 52–53; © James L. Stanfield/National Geographic Image Collection: pp. 2, 8–9, 12–13, 14–15, 34–35, 36, 74, 84–85, 92, 125, 142–143, 170–171, 187, 195, 221; © Janusz Rosikon: p. 75; © Kaku Kurita/Gamma: p. 144; © Periodici San Paolo: pp. 216–217, 219; © Maurizio Brambatti/Reuters/Piekna/MaxPPP: p. 44; © The Pierpont Morgan Library/Art Resource, NY. From *The Book of Hours of Catherine of Cleves*, Netherlands (Utrecht), c. 1435: pp. 22 (M.945, f.77v), 27 (M.945, f.35v), 71 (M.945, f.115v), 147 (M.917, f.72); © Servizio Fotografico de *L'Osservatore Romano*: pp. 32, 42–43, 63, 76, 80, 88–89, 99, 116 (right), 117, 124, 127, 130 (3 photos), 131, 137, 151, 155, 180, 192, 196, 207, 212 (top), 213, 215.

*In his study, Vatican City, 1986*

# ACKNOWLEDGMENTS

*An Invitation to Joy* was produced by Callaway Editions in collaboration with Leonardo Periodici.

Callaway Editions and Leonardo Periodici would like to give special thanks to Dr. Joaquín Navarro-Valls, Director of the Press Office of the Holy See; Don Giorgio Bruni, S.D.B.; the Servizio Fotografico de *L'Osservatore Romano*; Alberto Michelini; Jan Michelini; and Raoul Goff, Gordon Goff, and Erik Ko of Palace Press International.

Greg Burke would very much like to thank the following:

IN ROME

Archbishop Jorge María Mejía of the Vatican Library, Blandine Becheras, Caroline Bouan, Monsignor Arthur Calkins, Elizabeth Heil, Paolo Re, and Cindy Wooden.

IN MILAN AT LEONARDO PERIODICI

Gianni Gardel, Giorgio Gardel, and Marta L' Erede.

IN NEW YORK AT SIMON & SCHUSTER

Bill Rosen and Sharon Gibbons.

IN NEW YORK AT CALLAWAY EDITIONS

Nicholas Callaway, George Gould, Kenneth Kaiser, Paula Litzky, Toshiya Masuda, Monica Moran, Jeremy Ross, Tanya Semels, True Sims, Christopher Steighner, and Antoinette White.